Praise

Most of the Christian life happens i _____
the "long plains of faith." Chris Nye's *Distant God* helps us see the beauty in these long
"everyday" stretches, which may feel "meh" but are likely where most of our growth
will occur. Nye's book speaks a crucial word to our generation, reared on the authority
of experience and the sovereignty of emotion: God is here even when we don't feel
that He is. With the pastoral wisdom and eloquence of a young Eugene Peterson, Nye
reminds us that God's presence in our lives has more to do with obedience than feelings. A challenging, necessary call to me and my fellow millennials!

BRETT MCCRACKEN, journalist and author of *Hipster Christianity* and *Gray Matters*

Distant God is for when our faith has become frozen, and the path of discipleship
seems to pass by the dark side of the moon. Author Chris Nye gently walks aside the
reader, and with depth and wisdom points the way back to Christ, the divine light,
which warms our God-bathed world.

MARK SAYERS, lead pastor of Red Church, and author of *Facing Leviathan* and
Disappearing Church

It is so easy to quote Jesus' words "I am with you always" or speak "you are with me;
your rod and your staff, they comfort me" (Psalm 23:4), but what does that mean in
real life where "How long will you hide your face from me?" (Psalm 13:1) is a far more
common experience? Chris writes brilliantly and personally to help us find and live
God's presence. Rejoining God in His presence is not an easy work, but by the power
of the gospel, it is a good work for His people.

GERRY BRESHEARS, Western Seminary, Portland

The paradox is breathtaking. In a sense, God is mysteriously beyond us. Yet, God is
so unbelievably near to us. Both of these appear unable to live together. But they
must. As the faithful, we believe the binding that brings together God's nearness and
God's beyondness—Jesus Himself, God on a tree. While it's been said God is closer
to us than our next breath, we still forget to breathe. Within, Chris Nye's beautiful
exploration reminds us why we even breathe at all—for a chance to behold God's
ever-pressing grace.

A. J. SWOBODA, pastor, professor, and author of *The Dusty Ones* and *Introducing
Evangelical Ecotheology*

God sometimes seems so close that we can almost feel the divine breath on our necks.
But often, God seems like a ghost in the distance—blurry and noiseless. Chris Nye
reminds us that regardless of how we feel, God is *for* us, *in* us, *with* us. This book is
good news for all those who have reached for God and come up empty-handed.

JONATHAN MERRITT, author of *Jesus Is Better than You Imagined*

For too long the search for God's presence has been a for-mystics-only pursuit. In his book *Distant God*, Chris Nye not only aptly describes the emotional feeling of God being far off but also prescribes what drawing near Him in obedience can look like. Whether you sense God to be near or far, this book will be a helpful map for drawing closer to Him.

TYLER BRAUN, pastor and author of *Why Holiness Matters*

Christian Scripture and the Christian life are very much about being present with the Lord. In *Distant God*, Nye helps us see, understand, and feel this truth; but he does not stop there. Instead, Nye pushes this beautiful, biblical reality into our exceedingly distracted lives. Through grounded biblical practices and wisdom, Nye spotlights the importance of the presence of God and shows us divinely prescribed ways we can get there. *Distant God* is a gift to the church because it brings theology to life and into our lives. Nye has given us a work that cuts through the anxieties of our lonely, isolated generation and helps point us back to our only hope and solution, the God who draws near.

J. RYAN LISTER, author of *The Presence of God: Its Place in the Storyline of Scripture and the Story of Our Lives*

When I first heard the idea for this book, Chris Nye and I stood at the foot of a roaring waterfall in the Oregon woods. As I hold it now, I have the sensation that I felt then—of being in the presence of a dear and wise man, hearing him muse about a truth that could transform lives. *Distant God* leaps from the page with clear thought and seasoned wisdom. This book is pastoral and practical, open and grounded, awake to truth, biblically astute, and beautifully written. It will ground your mind, nourish your spirit, and open your eyes to the presence of God all around us. *Where is God?* Chris walks into that question honestly, as only a true pastor can. How happy I am that he has invited us to join him.

PAUL J. PASTOR, author of *The Face of the Deep: Exploring the Mysterious Person of the Holy Spirit*

Ah, those mountaintop spiritual experiences! Times when God's presence is overwhelming, undeniable. Alas, such moments are fleeting. Most of our days stretch out amid the mundane and routine—yet we never stop aching for another divine encounter, for more of God. Chris Nye is the perfect companion for our sojourn between the mountains. In *Distant God*, he combines pastoral wisdom with biblical insights to challenge popular assumptions about God's presence while pointing the way to a deeper, more meaningful relationship with our Maker. The result is an important book on a crucial topic from an author who demonstrates wisdom well beyond his years.

DREW DYCK, senior editor of CT Pastors and author of *Generation Ex-Christian* and *Yawning at Tigers*

DISTANT
GOD

CHRIS NYE

Why He feels far away . . .
and what we can do about it

MOODY PUBLISHERS
CHICAGO

© 2016 by
CHRIS NYE

Unless otherwise indicated, Scripture quotations are from the ESV® Bible (The Holy Bible, English Standard Version®), copyright © 2001 by Crossway, a publishing ministry of Good News Publishers. Used by permission. All rights reserved.

Scripture quotations marked NIV are taken from the Holy Bible, New International Version®, NIV®. Copyright © 1973, 1978, 1984, 2011 by Biblica, Inc.™ Used by permission of Zondervan. All rights reserved worldwide. www.zondervan.com. The "NIV" and "New International Version" are trademarks registered in the United States Patent and Trademark Office by Biblica, Inc.™

Scripture quotations marked NLT are taken from the Holy Bible, New Living Translation, copyright © 1996, 2004, 2007, 2013 by Tyndale House Foundation. Used by permission of Tyndale House Publishers, Inc., Carol Stream, Illinois 60188. All rights reserved.

Scripture quotations marked KJV are taken from the King James Version.

Edited by Jim Vincent   Cover design: Simplicated Studio
Interior design: Erik M. Peterson   Author photo: Jordan Chesbrough

Library of Congress Cataloging-in-Publication Data

Names: Nye, Chris (Pastor), author.
Title: Distant God : why he feels far away ... and what we can do about it / Chris Nye.
Description: Chicago : Moody Publishers, 2016. | Includes bibliographical references.
Identifiers: LCCN 2015050057 (print) | LCCN 2016006198 (ebook) | ISBN 9780802414373 | ISBN 9780802493941 ()
Subjects: LCSH: Hidden God. | Spiritual life--Christianity. | God (Christianity)--Knowableness.
Classification: LCC BT180.H54 N94 2016 (print) | LCC BT180.H54 (ebook) | DDC
231.7--dc23
LC record available at http://lccn.loc.gov/2015050057

We hope you enjoy this book from Moody Publishers. Our goal is to provide high-quality, thought-provoking books and products that connect truth to your real needs and challenges. For more information on other books and products written and produced from a biblical perspective, go to www.moodypublishers .com or write to:

Moody Publishers
820 N. LaSalle Boulevard
Chicago, IL 60610

1 3 5 7 9 10 8 6 4 2

Printed in the United States of America

To Ali,
for telling me to go for it

CONTENTS

"The trembling sense for the hereness of God is the assumption of our being accountable to Him. God-awareness is not an act of God being known to man; it is the awareness of man's being known by God. In thinking about Him we are thought by Him."

ABRAHAM JOSHUA HESCHEL

Part 1

MEASURING THE DISTANCE

ALL THE WAY down at the end of the dock, the inner tube Stu and I had occupied earlier now sits lonely as it glides atop the still water. My arms remain weak from holding on as the boat drags our small pre-teen bodies across the lake's glassy surface hour after hour. A full day like this in the sun causes the best of us to need a nap.

I decide to leap onto the tube once more. This time, there's no Stu, and I flip on my back and close my eyes. The sun fastens them shut, and before long the back and forth of the water rocks me to sleep.

Not even a half hour passes when I jolt awake to the sound of my name and find the once nearby dock now fifty feet away. I had drifted. Embarrassed, I began making the adjustments needed to head back to shore.

Chapter 1

THE LONGING
TO BE NEAR

How long, O Lord? Will you forget me forever?
How long will you hide your face from me?
PSALM 13:1

We know when God is near to us. Often, our stories about meeting Him line up with a memory of a remarkable feeling or sense that the Creator of Everything is somehow closer than He has ever been before. We're lying beneath a skyline of stars at night with friends, or driving along eternal open roads listening for something in the music blaring from our outdated car speakers, or walking outside on the third night of some summer camp in between nowhere and everywhere, calling out in a whisper and suddenly . . . He's there.

The minute we feel this presence of His, we seem to make two somewhat surprising conclusions: first, we know for certain *this must be God Almighty* and, secondly, we know that this is the way life is supposed to be always—with Him, in Him.

Pastors like me often are skeptical of these "feelings," and you may have heard one or two of us tell you that you shouldn't trust this "feeling" of yours, that faith is not about those sorts of things—you should get your head on straight and start learning some theology! Yes, that's what we say!

But what if moments where we felt close to God, however short and sweet they were, told us something true about being human? What if the glimpses of divine intimacy were invitations into becoming entirely whole? What if being fully human involved being fully wrapped up in something completely divine?

It's possible. But just because it's possible doesn't mean it's common, or that most of us take advantage of it, or ever take something like the presence of God seriously.

As I minister to my restless and anxious generation, I can't help but think that we must be missing God.

Most of what I deal with as a pastor involves people struggling to find, feel, experience, and know God. This is most of the job. A recent study says people come to church because they want to feel close to God and, as a pastor, many of those same people expect me to help them do just that. But how are they to know when they *do* find Him? And when they do find Him, how do they maintain the close proximity?

These are the questions Christians have wrestled with for years. There are no simple steps to rejoining God in His presence, no quick remedy for a heart that misses Him. But at the same time there are things people have done for thousands of years that help us push away the misconceptions of what it means to be near God and usher us into His entire reality. I am certain this conversation will continue on—it will and should keep going until long after we die. But as I minister to my restless and anxious generation, watch people at my bus stops staring at their phones, and read studies expounding on our collective loneliness, it becomes clear that my generation feels that they must be missing God . . . or something like Him.

Sometimes I'll be talking with someone at one of my church's Sunday services or meeting a student in our youth ministry for the first time, and it becomes painfully clear why they decided to come: they just want to talk to someone. Mother Teresa is famous for saying that the greatest epidemic in the world is not poverty or disease, but loneliness. I think people come to church for the same reason they sit up at night on Twitter or Netflix . . . they just need someone or something to be connected with.

LOOKING TO CONNECT WITH GOD

In our loneliness, we look to God for a connection too. Many students tell me they pray at night. I think this might be because that is their most lonely time. The friends are gone, the noise has quieted, and they lie in the dark, feeling the weight of their limitations as human beings.

Our prayers to God during these times are similar to texting a friend or seeing our phone buzz because we received attention on social media. Today, we want God to respond as instantaneously as our friends can, and when He doesn't, we are brought into despair. And so we wonder, *where is God when I need Him?*

But what should we expect of Him? Is this "presence" actually available to us in the way we would like in the twenty-first century? What if He never promised what we are hoping for? What if He promised something more than we hope for? Something better?

I was in eighth grade when I believe I first felt the weighty, terrifying, and peaceful presence of God. Theologians might call it God's "special" or "manifest" presence; some just call it "an encounter with the Holy Spirit." Whatever you want to call it, all I know is I *felt* something. I really cannot describe it, nor can many other Christians, at least very well. But at the core of my personhood, I felt more wicked and disgusting than ever before, but more loved than I had previously ever imagined—all at one time. The common reaction was *not* my normal go-to move: I cried. I do not know why I cried. In fact, at this particular moment, I was playing guitar in front of about seventy-five of my peers, helping lead worship, when it all happened.

I didn't know what to do, but I knew I couldn't be forever titled The-Kid-Who-Cried-Whilst-Playing-Crappy-Electric-Guitar-At-Camp—I would not stand for it! But I also seemingly could not tame this experience. And so, my declaration came when I set my guitar down, went into the front row, fell to the floor, and went about my crying.

I didn't cry for *that* long, but it was a solid, steady cry. After I settled down I was kind of in a trance, just thinking. I thought about my short life thus far and my life ahead, I thought about my friends, about girls, about my mom and dad and brother and sister and everything I'd ever read or heard about God, which, granted, wasn't much. As I sat there, listening to the music while the band I had just abandoned continued to play, I felt more alive than I ever had before.

When I came home from the trip, I had next to no idea what had exactly happened other than the fact that I believed I had encountered God. I grew up in a rather agnostic home without much exposure to Scripture and had been in Catholic school since early elementary school. I was perplexed by the concept of God meeting me in the way I had felt He did that night.

I can remember sitting over my dining room table with my mom, who had come back to her faith. She was asking me about the trip and I started to tell her about The Night. I remember precisely what I said. It's unfortunately important to mention here that, during this time in my life, I had been saving up and stocking massive amounts of music gear in my basement (and by "massive amounts," I mean a couple of pedals, amps, mics, and guitars). I thought I was building a "studio." For sure, I had a growing setup that I, as a young teenage boy, adored. And when I was telling my mom everything about The Night, I said something that even surprised *me*.

"Mom," I said, "I don't know what happened that night, but I know I would trade everything I own, all of my music stuff, to have it again."

And in many ways that's my story. Slowly over high school I did, in fact, sell or give away all of my music gear except for one guitar. I ditched my very feasible and practical idea of becoming a famous rock star (read that again, and make sure to add the sarcasm), dumped my eighth-grade girlfriend (whatever that meant and means to this day, I do not know), changed the high school I was planning on attending, and began my clumsy pursuit of God. Ever since then, I've been doing perhaps what you find yourself doing today: looking for Him again.

HOW POWERFUL IS THIS?

Is it possible that I misinterpreted my entire story? That I was just overly emotional and experiencing teenage angst and confusion, making up this whole God thing along the way? Did I change my entire life for some worthless and inconsequential adolescent experience?

I suppose it's *possible*.

But what if it's also possible that there is a divine resource, a God currently available to you and me, whom we are completely missing out on every day?

If you have never had a type of "religious experience," I can almost guarantee that someone you know has had something like it. In addition, it appears as though our Bibles are filled with stories of people encountering God and seeing their lives take new direction afterwards. For example, Abraham was married to a barren woman—near the end of his family line in a polytheistic community— when this One True God made Himself known. In fact, God's showing up in Abraham's life is the basis for three of the world's most important religious movements. Whether you're Jewish, Christian, or Muslim, all of us claim to be "children of Abraham," or descendants of a man who was changed because he was near to God and interacted with Him in some way, sensed His calling, and followed Him in what the Hebrews call "faith." It could be, and has been argued, that you really cannot expect to know much about most world civilizations without knowing something about this man, Abraham. He is responsible for most of human spirituality.

Did Abraham really interact with God? Was it really life changing? If he didn't, millions—billions, really—need to reevaluate their entire understanding of human life.

And these experiences are not just of old-school, biblical proportions. One of my best friends lives with his family in Turkey, where 98 percent of the population is Muslim. The young people in his city, Istanbul, grow up in a culture that promotes Islam and puts Christianity at a distance, claiming most of it as untrue. My friend works with missionaries, and the last time my wife and I visited him we sat in a café as I asked him how *anyone* in this kind of culture can be converted to Christianity.

"Dreams," he said simply as he sipped his Turkish tea. He went on to tell me that many of the converts in his church have had personal, relatable, powerful experiences with the presence of God either in a dream or in some strange vision. "Jesus appears to them . . . and they believe," he said shrugging. He acknowledged the bizarre nature of it all, but what are you going to say? These people have an experience with being near to this particular God—the God of Abraham, Isaac, and Jacob—and they change.

I remember after our trip my wife was reading a Christian

magazine that ran a cover story on people in the Middle East having an abnormal number of dreams where Jesus visited them. The writer said it was happening all over.

"Hey," my wife said.

"Yeah?" I replied.

"It's just like Istanbul." She was pointing at the cover.

Later, when I was in China, I met a man who was an artist. He painted beautiful landscapes of the Asian coastline and began telling me about them. As he explained each of them, he told me that he "sees the presence of God" when he paints his canvasses. When he gave me his business card, there was a small cross on the bottom left corner and, written in small Chinese letters, a Bible verse.

THE SPACIOUSNESS OF GOD

All of these stories (and countless others, certainly) are of course circumstantial, which is OK, because I'm not working to prove to you or myself that God's presence is real or that it has a certain power. "Prove" is the wrong word for what I'm trying to do; I'm just trying to get us to think about all of this.

If God isn't real, what are the religious doing? What are they feeling? Yes, of course, we can hook our brains up to monitors and see *how* it is happening and *where* in the brain it is going on, and even *what else happens* at that physical place in the brain under different circumstances. But all of that doesn't answer *why* it happens. *Why* is this science triggered? What sets it off? Why feel it *then* and not some other time? Just because we know *how* and *where* and *what* happens in our biological makeup doesn't mean we've automatically understood *why* our brains are responding and, in some cases, our whole trajectory of life changes after such experiences. This is because most of our experience happens not in our brains, but our minds.

There are these studies about silence and solitude I keep thinking about where people's brains actually begin to repair themselves just by sitting alone and meditating every day. Yes, their brains *repair themselves* by the simple spiritual practice of silence and meditation. There are also studies about how our brains light up in the strangest places when we're in worship services and when we pray with friends. As I said, we know *how* it happens and we know *where* it happens, but have you ever thought about *why* it happens?[1]

God is very spacious, and I believe He is interacting with more people and in more ways than you or your pastor or spiritual leader could tell you about. We live in what Dallas Willard would call a "God-Bathed World."[2] You and I do not just live in a "spiritual" world, but a world where "One Spirit" dominates and permeates all of existence, everywhere we go. God appears in the vastness of the ocean and the whispers of prayers; He is with us in our tears and alongside us as we laugh. There is no escaping God. As the psalmist asks, "Where shall I flee from your presence" (Ps. 139:7)?

And so this makes me think God is not isolated to these bizarre, seemingly once-in-a-lifetime religious experiences. Although He certainly *is* there in some special way, most of the time we are living in a world bathed in God's presence, and we are completely missing out on it. Instead our eyes lock with the screen on our phone and we miss Him. We see the worst in others and we miss Him. We stress about money and worry about time and fear death and watch TV and we miss Him. We experience the joy of a kiss and the pain of cancer and everything in between and we rarely talk to Him about it all—we do not believe He is involved or available in the midst of what we call "our life." I've got to wonder, in our hours of swiping our phones and mashing buttons on remotes and appliances while our world turns, is there any possibility we're not living awake to all of the things God is actually doing?

> We are living in a world bathed in God's presence and completely missing out on it.

There is nowhere that God is not, and yet, it seems we do not always recognize or seek Him. After we have these rare moments within God's space, we may want to go back, and can't. It's not enough for us to have had *one* great moment with Him or near Him like my moment in eighth grade, guitar in hand; we need to go back to Him again and again. Something about this presence comforts us, challenges us, and protects us all at once. I'm convinced that regular, everyday people experience something like this more than many Christians want to believe. God is active and present in more places than our churches want us to know. And there are more people—and perhaps this is you—who want to be let in again. And I think we can.

WHAT THE SCRIPTURES SAY
ABOUT GOD'S PRESENCE

"In your presence there is fullness of joy" says one psalmist in the Old Testament (Ps. 16:11). Another psalmist writes, "For me it is good to be near God" (73:28). And yet again, perhaps most famously, another writer of psalms declares, "My soul longs, yes, faints for the courts of the Lord" (84:2; "The courts of the Lord" is a way of saying, "Where God is"). In that same song, the writer declares, "A day in your courts is better than a thousand elsewhere. I would rather be a doorkeeper in the house of my God than dwell in the tents of wickedness" (v. 10).

Right alongside all of this, there are is equal or greater number of Psalms agonizing over God's absence: "How long . . . will you forget me?" cries the songwriter in Psalm 13:1. In speaking of the lack of God in his life, another writer says, "My tears have been my food" (Ps. 42:3). Remember the famous psalm, "My God, my God, why have you forsaken me?" (22:1; later quoted by Jesus on the cross)? What a profound yet sad song to be included in the Hebrew book of prayer.

In the New Testament, we see many moments of God's nearness to people. God appears to people and shows His glory to others (Matt. 3:16), speaks to people (Matt. 3:16–17; 17:5–6; Acts 13:1–3, 2 Cor. 12:7–9), and moves/works in people, imparting power and courage (see Stephen's Spirit-empowered speech in Acts 7).[3] The apostle Paul planted various churches and even has instructions for his congregations on how to deal with the God who is constantly speaking, working, moving, and revealing Himself through His Holy Spirit (1 Cor. 12–14, 1 Thess. 5:16–23).[4]

All of these support what you and I may feel or know from experience about God. We want to be near to Him; some would say, we *long* to be near and with God. We don't know much about Him; we're unclear on the projects He's running and His processes for accomplishing it all. Yet whether we call ourselves believers or not, there is a deep, dare I say *primal*, part of us that hopes for a time when the gap between us and this God could be closed. The truth for how all of this works together is complicated, as all those passages of Scripture I just cited suggest.

> The Scriptures seem to understand who we are and what we desire often better than we do.

The Bible seems to be filled with people who speak for us, who say, "Yes, God is *supposed* to be near. He is *supposed* to show up." Yes, all of us at times desire to be near God. And when we are near Him, it is good. Reading these Scriptures can be cathartic because they seem to understand who we are and what we desire oftentimes better than we do.

WHEN WE FEEL DISTANT FROM GOD

For those of us who have experienced this distance from God, I want to say this: it is real. We are justified in our *feeling* of being far from God. I think, in many ways, this is an essential part of being human. To feel dissatisfied with our relationship with God and to not be OK with our proximity to Him might be a gift from God Himself. As French mathematician and philosopher Blaise Pascal wrote in his classic *Pensees*: "There was once in man a true happiness [when Adam and Eve first walked with God, without sin. Today every human] . . . tries in vain to fill with everything around him, . . . though none can help, since this infinite abyss can be filled only with an infinite and immutable object; in other words by God himself."[5]

But at the same time, we must examine this emotional distance from God and put it under a kind of prayerful microscope. Our desires change and are usurped by other wants and needs deep within our hearts. As these things come up, we medicate in different ways, and the longing for God slowly goes away—and we should emphasize the *"slowly"* part, right? Day by day, it's like growing up in reverse, you never feel it or know it's happening until you take the time to measure it. And sometimes, when we finally take the time to measure where we are at with God— as we look at the communion meal, or hear a sermon, or hear a song about Him—the damage is already done. It's as if we have drifted from a dock; all of a sudden we no longer see land.

THE LONG PLAINS OF FAITH

When I began my journey with God, many people told me about the "mountaintop" moments of faith. They told me how we get moments high above the normal horizon of life to be closer to Him. Some people even told me that camps and retreats were "thin places" where heaven and earth sort of meet. I liked that.

But people also told me about the "valleys" of faith and life, how times of trouble bring us into deep caverns of doubt, disbelief, and depression. I can remember when my parents were getting divorced; some years later, when I was nineteen, my leaders told me this was a season where I would have to just keep walking, because maybe a "mountaintop" was in the future. I liked this too; it helped me a great deal.

But nobody told me about the long stretches in between the mountains and valleys. No one told me that most of my life in faith would be painstakingly ordinary and benign. No one mentioned tales of the long, grassy plains of faith— the eternal highways of straight paths where you struggle to stay awake at the wheel and hope for the rest stop promised miles before.

In his famous novel *On the Road*, Jack Kerouac wrote about how you never really know how big America is until you drive across it. I have felt this several times on different trips through California or the Midwest. Once, while making our way to Wyoming, my family and I spent an entire day without taking a single turn. For eight to ten hours, my father kept the wheel steady. I stared out the window of the RV we had rented to see the landscape of our country. Everything was moving, but nothing was changing. It reminds me of faith sometimes.

I tend to have more days like this than days where I felt like I was at the top of Everest or near the bottom of any great American valley. Life with God is not always extreme. Faith is not just about "mountaintops and valleys." It also involves traffic jams and long stretches of unexciting freeways.

Everything was moving but nothing was changing. It reminds me of faith sometimes.

These are precisely the times we lose God. As a pastor, I notice most of those who tell me about their dissatisfaction with God are in a very *normal* time in their life. Rarely will someone complain of feeling distant from God after a camp or missions trip, or a time of great suffering. Mostly, those unsure about where God is in all of it are in the routine of daily work, whether it's school or their nine-to-five job.

My story involves learning how to relate with God during the long plains of faith. While I've experienced the mountains and the valleys—death, debt, disease, and the divorce of my parents—I've also mostly experienced long stretches of time that lack anything special. And so it has become necessary to develop a theology—an understanding of God—that reflects this precise experience. What do we do with a God who seemingly goes away? Does He really do that?

If we think that life with and in God's presence is a beautiful, life-giving thing, and the people in the Bible seem to talk quite positively about it, then why are we not experiencing it all the time? What's wrong? Are the communication lines broken on our side or His? And if the break is on His side, what did we do?

Chapter 2

WHO IS THE DISTANT ONE?

Happiness does not consist of . . . being like God so much as it does being with God.[1]
JOHN SAILHAMER

We were folding tables and stacking chairs after one of our midweek summer gatherings for high school students when Michelle approached me hesitantly.

"Can I talk to you for a second?" she asked.

"Sure," I said. "What's going on?"

"You know Corey, right?"

"I do."

"I'm a little worried about him," she said, looking away.

That's when Michelle began a very familiar conversation with me. Corey, she explained, was ready to "give up on the whole God thing." He'd look around the youth group and our church and see people experiencing God in worship, seemingly passionate about their pursuit, and he couldn't relate. He'd been doing devotionals in the morning, praying a little bit, and coming to church. Why does he not feel close to God? What more must he do?

Michelle told me Corey was ready to throw in the towel and let the Christians be Christians. It wasn't for him.

I appreciated Michelle's concern, and unfortunately her fears were well-founded. I have had far too many conversations with young people about their dissatisfaction with their nearness to God. Is Corey right? Should he give up?

The truth is, people do so all the time. People abandon God without ever knowing Him or even understanding the nuances to this vital faith that has sustained the souls of men and women, teens, and children for thousands of years. For those who abandon God, most believe God has abandoned their expectations, and they see no reason to continue pursuing a God who will let them down.

And I don't blame them. Their expectations have been dashed. But that's the problem—we have expectations of God that are wrapped in our view of Him. That view is based on our understanding of who He is, *His nature*. This is called "theology." Our theology creates our expectations of God, and it seems as though the issues surrounding our distance from God are tied to what we think God *should* do. So let's go on a little journey.

THE SETUP

No matter what you believe about the first couple, Adam and Eve, we cannot talk about the distance between us and God and how to repair it without talking about those two. In their story we find our story; in their fall from God, we can see ours as well. While our particular words and interactions may change, the heart within the story of the very first couple seemingly plays out in our lives every day—both seen and unseen. It is startling how often I see this story continue to play out in my own life and the lives of those in my church family. We need to look deeply into this story for us to gain insight into our God and us.

At the very start of the book of Genesis, in a garden called Eden, all of the relationships those two human beings had were in harmony. The relationships between the two, God, and creation (including the animals), were "good" according to the Creator. Before Eve appeared, God and Adam were colaborers working together and conversing (2:15–17), delegating work to each other and seeing the world grow. God created man intimately by placing His hands in the ground and blowing air into his lungs. The Genesis story says that He placed Adam in the garden to work it and keep it (v. 15). This God is not distant and far removed in the Genesis story, but rather *with* Adam in his daily life.

In Adam's proximity to God he is working, going about the business of ordinary life in a particular geographic place. Adam is near to God—relating with Him and conversing and obeying. The *shalom*—peace of God—is alongside the mundane atmosphere of a garden and a man. Together, God and man are working out this *shalom* in Eden. For us to expect to have more than this in our current time may prove to bring us great disappointment. Our nearness to God entails working with Him in the ordinary stuff of life.

Our nearness to God entails working with Him in the ordinary stuff of life.

God provides everything for Adam in the garden, including a wife. God is intimate in His creative process, taking the rib of the man to fashion the woman. They stand before each other and God without any shame, and their marriage is made in the presence of their Creator. Farming, working, naming, marrying, all happen in the presence of God. All is right.

As we view this scene, it can be tempting for us to believe what perhaps some Bible teachers have taught us, that Eden is "perfect." Perfect is maybe the wrong word for Eden—God didn't use this word. Eden was a place God arranged for the flourishing of His relationships with image bearers (humans), where they could together work out the *shalom* to the rest of the earth. Eden was "good," according to God (Gen. 1). This entire situation is, as a professor of mine told me, "incomplete." Eden was certainly a "good" place, but it was not complete. Was there a possibility to disobey and rebel during this time in human history? Absolutely.

THE STORY OF SIN

For Adam and Eve—yes, for us too—being *with* God is often not enough. Rather, when the temptation comes to be *like* God in exchange for being *with* Him, often we take it. Being with God is fine for us, but if we can have some sort of power like a god, if we can be wise instead of foolish, rich instead of poor, and happy instead of possibly sad, many of us will abandon the presence of the Almighty. That exchange is all too easy for us (and this first couple) to make.

God asks His image bearers to refrain from eating of one tree in the garden (v. 17). This tree, by all accounts in the text, contains no magic in and of itself. It is not correct for us to say it is a special tree because the Scriptures do not say it had some sort of hidden spiritual power. Rather, God placed the tree in the garden in order for man to have pure trust in the Creator. God places this tree in the garden as if to say, "I want you to do something only because I told you to . . . no other reason."

As many others have noted, it is important we remember this was not the *only* tree in the garden of Eden. In fact, the first couple was told they could eat from any other tree in this fruitful garden (v. 16). In this moment, they (like us) have many options, and yet (once again, like us) they choose to do the opposite of what God commands them to do.

We must ask ourselves, are we trusting God and allowing Him to define what is right and wrong, good and bad? Or, would we like to make that decision ourselves? The first couple wanted to do what we still want to do: put matters in our own hands.

The power of God's words and narrative ("do not eat . . . you shall surely die") is usurped by the Serpent's lies ("eat . . . you will not die"). All the Serpent has to do to us is put a question mark on the end of God's commands: "Did God actually say?" (3:1). To this day, we can hear the voice of the Serpent infiltrating our minds. You always know the voice of the enemy when he puts question marks where God has put periods.

"What kind of God is he if he tells you to do that?"

"Forgive? Now?"

"Why would a *loving* God command *that?*"

"Do not lie? Really? Everyone has to lie at some point."

"*Love* your enemy? That doesn't seem realistic in this situation."

"It's not *that* bad, is it?"

We are more intimate with this voice than the Almighty's. This is the voice we have come to know so well—we've even learned to trust it, to rely on its invitations and comfortable feelings. We rest in this voice because it normally unearths our own desires for self-satisfaction and gain. To this day, the Serpent changes the punctuation and emphasis in God's sentences.

Famously, Adam and Eve give in to the temptation and choose the word of the Serpent over the word of God— they exchange the truth for a lie (see Rom. 1:25), one story for another story. The initial consequence of fulfilling self-ishness is always shame, and this is what comes to our first couple. When we are ashamed of something we've done, we hide. But what happens next?

"And they heard the sound of the Lord God walking in the garden in the cool of the day, and the man and his wife hid themselves from the presence of the Lord" (Gen. 3:8). The next verse has incredible significance: "But," the author of Genesis writes, "the Lord God called to the man and said to him, 'Where are you?'"

THE GOD WHO PURSUES US

When we sin, we hide.

But . . .

When we sin, *God seeks*.

The last thing we feel like doing in our misdoings and sinning is to seek God. And yet, from the very first sin, we see a God who pursues us even as we are disobeying Him. This is, after all, the entire arch of Scripture's metanarrative in Christ. We must understand this fundamental concept.

There is a common phrase in Christianity, and it goes something like this: "God cannot be in the presence of sin." We use examples of pure water and putting a little bit of rat poison in it, and we say, "That's not pure water!" But this speaks to God's *uniqueness* toward sin, but not his presence among it. Where do we get this teaching from? Surely God can be in the presence of sin; we're reading about it in Genesis 3 right now! Furthermore, who is Jesus? A friend—no, a God—among sinners and "bearing the sins of the world" on the cross.

I've heard a lot of preachers and speakers mention this line from Genesis 3:8 (God was "walking in the garden in the cool of the day") as a way to talk about the relationship between God and man *before the fall*. But this line about God taking a walk among His image bearers comes *after the fall*. God certainly has the ability to be in the presence of sin, for that is where His best work can happen. God's holiness does not exclude Him from working in sin and in us, but rather His perfection moves Him toward sin to cleanse us, heal us, and make everything new.

From the very first story of the very first human beings, we can understand God does not limit His presence because of sin. It is not that simple. The story is more complex and involves us more than we would like. We want the story to be a simple one where God just can't be around any sin, so He leaves. But the truth is more complicated. His holiness motivates Him. While God seeks us in our sin, our sin still ruins our relationship with Him (cf. 2 Tim. 2:13).

THEIR STORY AND OUR STORY

In Adam and Eve's sin, God seeks and asks the profound question: *"Where are you?"* A beautiful statement filled with massive implications. Did God ask this question of Adam because He did not know where Adam was? We can, I believe, safely assume this not to be the case. Rather, God asked this question because *Adam* did not know where he was.

When God is far away, it is not uncommon for us to ask this same question of Him. "Where are You, God?" I do not believe this to be a detrimental or negative thing to ask or pray. The psalmist asks this question, as do many people throughout Scripture (e.g. Job 23:31; Ps. 13:1). However, as we ask this question, we also must consider God to be asking this of us. Do we know where *we* are? When we sense the presence of God moving away from our lives, have we even located ourselves on the map before we begin our search for God? We may, as we examine our lives, find ourselves in the bushes covering ourselves up.

Our own sin and shame bring us into hiding. We may

be reading our Bible and praying, but if our lives remain unchanged with calloused hearts, our devotions may be unfruitful. There's this strange verse where, after Peter outlines commands for the Christian husband and wife, he tells men to "live with your wives in an understanding way . . . so that your prayers may not be hindered" (1 Peter 3:7). Just one chapter later, he says, "Be self-controlled and sober-minded *for the sake of your prayers*" (1 Peter 4:7, emphasis added). These verses seem to line up with the famous passage in 2 Chronicles 7 on prayer: "If my people . . . humble themselves, and pray . . . *and turn from their wicked ways*, then I will hear from heaven" (v. 14). There seems to be a strange link between our prayers and our actions—and we need to carefully consider it.

There are times when God does not hear our prayers. I cannot put it more plainly, albeit painfully. As we seek God and ask for His presence, we must first hear His voice: "Where are you?" We cannot continue to walk through Christian religious motions without locating ourselves on the map of obedience and repentance. Have we been walking outside of the commands of God in wickedness, mistreating our loved ones and working for selfish gain? Our lifestyle could be leading us to the shrubs away from the presence of God Himself.

As we locate ourselves, we know God's Word does not end here. In response to this question, Adam *does* tell the truth, even if it is an incomplete truth: "I heard the sound of you in the garden, and I was afraid, because I was naked, and I hid myself" (Gen. 3:10). There is nothing false about this statement. In fact, this is a good confession, and Adam is telling God the truth. But he is insecure in his identity with God, which is why he mentions his nakedness.

Notice, God has not poured judgment upon Adam at all. We cannot miss the expansive grace in this story. Over and over, God is seeking, asking, and allowing both Adam and Eve to repent and seek forgiveness from the One who can freely give it. No wrath. No curse. Just a conversation. God is doing what He always does with us: in grace, there is an offering of repentance.

> God is seeking, asking . . . doing what He always does with us: in grace, there is an offering of repentance.

"Who told you that you were naked? Have you eaten of the tree of which I commanded you not to eat?" (v. 11). Ah, a specific question. Yet again: is God asking this because He does not know? It is difficult to answer this with an affirmative because we know God to be all-knowing. Again, God is asking this question for Adam's sake, not His. God is offering a chance for repentance. Adam decides to do what you and I do so often: shift the blame and make excuses.

"The woman you gave to me . . ."

In one sentence, Adam plays the victim and blames both God and the woman. It is quite the accomplishment. Notice all of the moments God offers a chance for Adam to repent and turn—to honestly confess and receive the grace of God. Adam is asked multiple questions. Most of us tell the story like this: the couple knew not to eat the fruit (2:16–17; 3:2–3), they ate the fruit, and God banished them from the garden. But this is not what happens. After the couple sins, God seeks them out and offers them a chance to tell the truth. Adam's failure is not just in eating the fruit; Adam's failure is in his inability to take responsibility for his sin, to confess and repent.

God turns to the woman and gives the same offering of possible repentance: "What is this that you have done?" He asks.

Eve replies, "The serpent deceived me, and I ate."

The couple now receives consequences for their choice to live against the ways of God, and the troubling story of humanity begins. The story of the beginning of the world is not a story of good versus evil, but a story of a good world God made and the rebels within it. We are still in a place where God asks us questions not for His benefit, but for ours. This is not a war of good vs. evil; this is a civil war.

As rebels, God banishes them from the place He created for their flourishing. He moves them to the east of Eden and places a flaming sword at the entrance—meaning, the only way back in to the garden would be through death, to go through the sword. Now the separation occurs, and our feelings resonate with the couple.

Our sin has brought us to a place where relating with God is a difficult process. For most of us, the word "sin" is connected only to behavior. We use the word to say things like, "I sinned," or, "I'm trying not to sin." But the reality of sin is that it is a cancer, a disease we are ridden with, which makes us desire ourselves and not God. We are infected, and this infection has complicated the relationship between us and God. Things are not as simple as we would like them to be, and this cancerous, destructive disease has separated us from God. He continues to seek us, but we cannot continue in our sin.

How do we find Him again?

FROM THIS SIDE OF HISTORY

When Jesus of Nazareth comes on the scene opening the kingdom of heaven to the poor in spirit, the meek and persecuted, we can, from our current perspective, see what God was doing all along. In Christ, God was accomplishing a major initiative in His mission: reopening Eden (Rom. 5:12–21; Rev. 22:1–5).

Because Jesus went through the flaming sword for us, we can now reenter the garden to know God and His Holy Spirit by His grace. The consequences of sin are lifted by the Deliverer. Putting it another biblical way, the veil has been lifted and the temple curtains have been torn in two. Through Christ, our access has been granted into the Holiest of Holies, and our communion with God need not be done through a temple, festivals, and the law. Now through Christ Himself, we can come to the Father. This is the staggering reality of the New Testament, particularly the book of Hebrews.

But how come you and I do not relate with this teaching as much as the Genesis 3 teaching? How come we, despite our benefits received through Christ and the new covenant, continue to feel exiled from Eden?

In my pastoral work, my appointments include more exiles of Eden than citizens of it—at least, according to how they see themselves. We have been given the revelation of God in Christ. We do not need Moses to go up to the mountain for us, but rather, God has come down the mountain in Christ. However, even though we have the all-access pass, even though the kingdom of heaven—the community where God rules—is "in our midst," it seems like it doesn't always work the way we think that it should.

> Like our ancestors Adam and Eve, we are filled with shame . . . We hide ourselves and make as many excuses as we can.

Instead, we are like our ancestors Adam and Eve. We are filled with shame at what we have and have not done. We hide ourselves and make as many excuses as we can. We go deep into unhealthy relationships so the loneliness goes away, we pursue careers and make money to hide who we really are, and we keep going to church in order to make things feel OK, but they don't. We know how it *should* be, and it is not that way.

Yesterday I met with this student of mine who described his faith as "drifting" and "floating" with little to no direction. "Everything is right up here," he said as he pointed to his head, "but nothing's happening here," and he moved his hand to his heart. This is what it feels like to be lost. We know intellectually that we should not be where we are, but getting ourselves out is an entirely different process that will involve more than we know—more than our minds. No matter what, we must understand that it is not God who is the one who leaves, but us.

Perhaps, like Adam, we need to take some time to locate ourselves. Maybe you're like Corey, who I told you about at the start of this chapter. You pray and read your Bible, you go to church and listen to sermons, you sing worship songs, and after all of that you sit back and realize you're not really sure where God is in the middle of it all. Maybe, like Adam, you need to turn the question you've been asking God back on to yourself: *"Where are you?"*

Chapter 3

FINDING OUT WHERE YOU ARE

Sin is a hard heart and a stiff neck.[1]
CORNELIUS PLANTINGA JR.

I want to remind you of a story that has been so over-told I'm actually unsure how to approach it. If you have grown up in the church, it is most likely you have heard this story so many times you could probably retell it in a better way than I can. So let me start with this: put down this book and go reread Luke 15.

You know Luke 15? Let me jog your memory: Luke 15 includes the parable of the prodigal son—or, as pastor Timothy Keller would put it: the parable of the prodigal *sons*, plural. Their story is very helpful for what we're talking about. When we talk about God's nearness and distance, I'd like for us to remember these boys.

OK—did you read this story in Luke 15? The younger son becomes estranged from God because of rebellion. He runs away and spends all his inheritance money because he does not do what his father had planned for him. The older son becomes estranged from his father because of his rights. One loses God by running; the other loses Him by staying. At different points in the story, both sons feel the loss of a father, which is the feeling we get when we do not sense God being near.

When we hear God ask, *"Where are you?"* to us and to Adam in Genesis 3:9, I wonder if these two sons can help us formulate an answer.

THE YOUNGER BROTHER: REBELLION

We're far more comfortable and familiar with the story of the younger son. I've heard many stories in my church matching up perfectly with the rebellious brother. I think about Stanley (not his real name), a father of a couple of students in my youth ministry who spent years outside of any realization that God was good and cared about him. In Stanley's words, "I gave God and the world the middle finger for years." You've heard a story like Stanley's too: substance abuse, unhealthy relationships, unstable life, and some illness or hurt.

What happens next to the younger brother? "He came to his senses" (v. 17 NIV) is what Jesus says about the younger brother, and he comes home to his father.

This flavor of rebellion is often where people come from before they land in a church. It's a sad story with a beautiful ending. But there's also another kind of rebellion, and it goes like this . . .

I'm sitting with one of my leaders over coffee and I'm a

little anxious because we're making small talk, but I know this meeting has a lot more involved in it than talking about the Portland Trailblazers. His text read: "I've got some stuff on my mind. Can we meet up soon?" and so I break the courtesies:

"Why did you want to talk?" I ask him.

This leader tells me he needs to step down from leadership. This is fine by me because I always have leaders stepping in and out with youth ministry; it's part of the job.

"Why? Everything OK?" I ask.

"Yeah. . . ." He pauses. "I'm just not feeling passionate about it and I think I need some time to focus on me," he says.

"Time to focus on me," hangs in my mind as I think through the unfortunate reality of that statement. This is what it means to be an American: to focus on ourselves. What my leader does not know is that he is stepping into a trap. To focus on ourselves is to lose our very life.

"Whoever loses his life for my sake," Jesus told His disciples, "will find it" (Matt. 16:25). Jesus teaches us the exact opposite of what our culture encourages. The irony is that the very moment we focus on ourselves is the moment we begin losing everything about us. We were never meant for self-absorption, but self-giving.

> We were never meant for self-absorption, but self-giving.

This self-absorption and focusing on ourselves is the subtle rebellion of the twenty-first century. This is all the younger brother was doing—and the elder brother, for that matter. There is no faster way to move away from God

43

than to move further in on yourself. The manifestation of self-absorption can be drugs and sexual promiscuity for sure, but it can also involve greed and pride in its most understated, acceptable forms.

What pained me about my conversation with my leader who needed to step down was not that he felt exhausted with ministry—exhaustion is in ministry's very essence. What broke my heart was how he had bought the lie that he just needed a little more time to do what he wanted to do. In this process, he would begin losing God. It was only a matter of time before I stopped seeing him at church and my texts went unanswered.

In rebellion, our go-to move is justification. We start managing our life because we think we deserve certain things for all of our hard work and loyalty. The younger brother asked for his inheritance early because he thought he deserved to not only receive it, but to do whatever he wanted with it whenever he wanted. Doing whatever we want whenever we want is the heart of rebellion, and we'll say anything to anyone in order to continue doing what we want to do.

We will play the blame game and tell people "the church" is the problem and we find God in our own way, charting our own path. We will start finding every reason not to submit to any authority, find teachers and pastors who will tell us our vices are not sinful and our selfish behavior is something we've earned. Any justification will do.

We must commit to not do the things *we* want to do, but instead do the things *He* has asked us to do. We have to "come to our senses," as the younger brother did, and head home. The open arms of the Father await us. This is what it means to humble ourselves before God.

THE OLDER BROTHER: RIGHTS

The older brother is trickier. His story is more nuanced and complex because he is living in the comfort of his father's house and remained obedient to his father. After his brother comes home and is celebrated for his safe return, the older sibling insists he didn't get what he deserved. In his mind, he had done all he needed to, he had served and given and done all the things he was told, and no one congratulated him. He had a right to a celebration, he thought, and did not receive any pats on the back.

Again, as Americans and sinners this is our other default mode. We have become accustomed to defend our rights, to stand up for them, and to believe we are always in the right. We become experts at seeing how people are ruining our "right to happiness" or "not supporting us" and, becoming incessantly insecure, we lose track of our standing in God's house.

In standing up for our rights, our go-to move is entitlement. Both brothers actually do this in different ways. And for us, we start noticing how other people are treated and we wonder why we aren't treated the same way or better. We start rewarding ourselves because "we have been good" and we begin to be steadfast in showing people we're good by standing up for what we believe in—in our "rights." The strange irony is we end up being enslaved by those rights.

The only way out of entitlement is to do what Jesus did.

Jesus never stood up for His rights—He laid them down. Paul says He "did not count equality with God a thing to be grasped." In other words, Jesus didn't hold on to His rights as God (Phil. 2:6). During His time on earth, Jesus was tempted several times to save Himself, prove His divinity, and call down the angels of heaven; yet He did not. Why? Because Jesus rested in His secure relationship with His Father. He didn't need to prove it with a big party because He was already living in the house with all of the heavenly resources available to Him.

THE FATHER'S HEART

This story of two brothers concludes with this final line of the Father to the older son: "You have always been with me and all that I have is yours." That verse has recently captured me as I think about God's presence and our distance from Him.

Many of us are looking around for God in His own house. We forget that we have the resources we need to find Him again sitting all around us. As we'll see in the next chapter, His presence has a lot to do with our attention to it. We lose God often because we lose our awareness of Him. This is precisely what both brothers lost as well, for when a person clings to their rights or explores the wilderness of rebellion, they become less aware of God.

The truth is, both brothers became unsatisfied with always being with their father and having all of his resources—they both wanted out and decided to take things into their own hands instead of doing the difficult work of gratitude. Whether you are in a place of rebelling from whatever God wants or in a place where you feel entitled to your rights with God, it may be in your best interest to remind yourself . . .

"You are always with me, and all that is mine is yours" (Luke 15:31).

Can we speak this to ourselves? Is this something we can memorize and recite when we are struggling with the allure of things outside of the house or when we become dissatisfied with the many things our soul can ache over? Can we say this when we're singing a song at church we hate, or when we don't want to read our Bibles, or when we're going to work for the eighth day in a row and cannot stand the sight of the place again? Can we speak this over our souls in a prophetic way that reminds us of who we are and—maybe more importantly and profoundly—*where we are already*?

BE CAREFUL NOT TO ASSUME

When I first started dating Ali, I was eighteen. When you're eighteen, you do a lot of work to try and convince people you are a certain type of person. I wanted people to believe I was creative. I carried around little notebooks and always had an interesting novel nearby to showcase either on the bus or at work. In the early season of our relationship, I did a lot of things to try and prove I was worth her time. I bought her flowers, told her things that were sort of true and deeply true, wrote songs for her to show my feelings because I couldn't always speak them, and tried to pay for her when we went out. I was, by all accounts of my memory, pathetic.

While I have grown up a bit since then, I still do things for Ali like this. As her husband, in order to maintain the relationship, it is important for me to buy her things, tell her my feelings, and take her on dates each week I can. While she and I have matured over time, it would not be healthy for me to abandon everything I did when I was first in love with her. The things I did for Ali when we were younger may have been a bit juvenile, but they were nevertheless acts of love toward her. They may not have been the best, but they were *something*.

I sometimes hear of people talking about God like a phase. They'll say things like, "That was when I was a Jesus Freak," or make mention of a time when they took things with God "too seriously." When we do this, we forget Jesus has always wanted us to be His children playing in His house. Unfortunately, we have a distorted self-view and believe ourselves to be too old for such child's play.

The worst relationships operate out of assumption. I see people do this all the time with God. They pray a prayer (maybe), have a moment with Him (maybe), go on a trip or camp (maybe), and then they just do whatever they want, assuming "God will forgive me" and "God will love me anyways." Well, of course He will love you anyways, but will you love Him anyways? Probably not. This is why it is important to lay down our rights, to repent, to obey, to move ourselves out of rebellion and into the house where everything God has can be ours. God is asking us to enter in to the party He is throwing.

BE CAREFUL TO BE ASSURED

And yet, as we are careful to not make assumptions about where we are at with God, we must be assured that God is near to us. Our attention to the good news of Jesus—that His work has brought us into the family of God forever—will bring us the assurance we need: we are in the house of the Father and we are always with Him and everything He has is ours.

I think for a lot of us we stand outside of our Father's house unsure if we're welcome or debating whether we want to go in. For the rebellious bunch, we contemplate the vast areas of life left undiscovered. We're always thinking we're missing out on a life God cannot possibly offer us. We see our social media feed buzzing with activities that we can't believe we're missing out on, and we think this whole God thing is keeping us back from a life He could never give us. So we ask for everything up front and begin praying prayers like, "God, this is Your last chance to prove Yourself . . . " We take the money and run.

Those of us with entitlement, holding on to our rights within God's house, begin complaining about our churches, about the people we start seeing in leadership or in the baptismal. We quickly become frustrated with "people" and "church" as opposed to doing the hard work of reconciling with particular names and faces. We generalize. We judge. We distance ourselves and begin to wonder, *Why don't people "get it?"*

All the while, we stand outside of the Father's house. Some of us rake the leaves in the front yard or watch people come and go, but we stay outside trying to prove to our-selves, and maybe Him, that we belong there. Some of us have a past of rebellion and think we could never enjoy the spoils of the mansion. We do all of these mental and spiritual gymnastics only to have the Father say, *"You were always with me, and everything I have is yours."*

BEING SURE

The book of Hebrews says that faith can be defined as "confidence in what we hope for and assurance about what we do not see" (11:1–2 NIV). Faith is about *knowing*. And "knowing" is both relational and factual. It is about being *sure* we belong to God and reminding ourselves of the work *God has done* to bring us into His family forever. Earlier in the same letter, the writer warns his readers, "We must pay much closer attention to what we have heard, lest we drift away from it" (2:1). When I talk with students of mine or hear people describe their fading relationship with God, I hear the word "drift" a lot.

Growing up, my best friend Stuart and his family would take us to Priest Lake in northern Idaho. We would often go in the middle of July when the temperatures were in the 90s, and most of our days would be spent enjoying the refreshing, cool waters of the lake. I can still see Stuart's dad pulling us for hours behind his boat on water skis and tubes.

Many days, after hours being thrashed about behind the speedboat, we would pull up near the shore and lay on the tubes to relax, feeling the heat of the sun drying us off. It was not uncommon for me to fall asleep briefly at the shore's edge and then wake up to someone yelling. As I awoke from my sunny daze, I (more than once) discovered I had moved much farther away from the shore than I realized. When I stopped paying attention to the shore, I drifted.

Have you ever felt this way? Are you feeling this way now? There was a time—and maybe it was not too long ago—where we were *sure* God loved us and *certain* His work in our lives and in human history was changing us. We *knew* God was near. But then . . . a drift happened. We stopped looking at Him, gazing at His Word and sensing His love. It was slow, to be sure. But all of a sudden we found ourselves far from shore—far from home and uncertain if we belonged back there. How do we obtain this certainty again?

When we drift, our problem is that we are not entirely sure from where we are drifting. What I mean is, I've discovered a lot of us who don't know what "the shore" even looks like. To put this in the metaphor of the sons in the house of the father: we have no idea what home is.

For most of us, this shore or home is a *feeling*. When we first met God, we *felt* a certain way. We were at a camp, a missions trip, or in a particular church service when we felt the peace of God. Following Him for the next week after that was effortless. And so we work the rest of our lives to get back to that *feeling*. But when the feeling doesn't come, we become disappointed and unsure if this whole God thing is real. *Were we just making everything up?*

For others of us, our home is a fixed set of moral code, and we're always paying attention to our behavior and what we're not doing right. When we stop doing the right thing, we consider ourselves drifting and "one of those hypocritical Christians." After a while, we give up and think there's no way *anyone* can continue such a strict code. We don't want to continue missing the mark of perfection, and so we change our target, adopt new morals, and throw the "God" thing away with it all.

But what if our targets, shores, and homes need adjusting? I'm convinced our generation is in need of some serious correction when we talk about God and His presence. "I don't feel close to God" is a loaded statement with tons of assumptions and expectations—do you ever wonder if some of them might be off base? Sometimes I wonder how many of us are thinking incorrectly about God. Are we right to be expecting a *feeling* of closeness to God at all times? Does the Bible teach or show this? How can we be sure God is near?

We do not worship sensation or experience. We worship Jesus. As I read Scripture and see what our generation says about God's presence, I believe we are in need of changing our expectations for what we (and God) can and cannot do about this problem of God's distance.

Chapter 4

ADJUSTING OUR EXPECTATIONS

The knowledge that we are never alone calms the troubled sea of our lives and speaks peace to our souls.[1]

A. W. TOZER

I'm sitting in a park, trying to read the pages I have failed to finish before my seminary class on a Thursday, when I see a young father scoop up his small son in his arms. Laughing, the child relaxes his entire body as his father tosses him into the air. As just an observer, I can see the love between the two of them increase as their play and communal joy brings them together. Before this moment, this little boy was the son of this father. But during this moment, they are more father and son than ever before.[2]

Relationships exist on a moving spectrum; they are anything but static. Our relationship with God is as real of a relationship as a father has with a son. As we come to join God's family, we are adopted as sons and daughters—this is our new familial status. And yet, just like earthly family, we can become estranged or enveloped, near or far, and as we continue through different experiences in life, our intimacy can change. The boy and his father I saw in the park did not live in a state of perpetual joy together, but moments of joy came out of living a life together.

THE PRESENCE OF GOD

One can be with someone and yet not near the person. *Presence* can be a slippery term. In one sense, presence is just about physical proximity, the location of a person or thing. To be in the presence of your mother is to have her in the room.

But then there's the presence that comes with some weight or gusto. This is the kind of presence you may have felt from your first crush as he or she turned the corner into the class you were sitting in, or the first time you saw that band you love in concert. It is one thing when someone is close by, it's another thing when someone important is near.

With our parents, there are times when you would come home from school, throw your backpack on the ground, grab something from the fridge, and pass your parents without much of an interaction. But then there were times you *knew* they were near and their presence mattered. From the complete joy of being tossed in the air as a child or having the hammer of discipline come down, parents have a way of making their presence not just known, but felt. It wasn't always up to us, was it?

Every relationship goes through bouts of closeness and distance, and our relationship with God exists on a somewhat similar level. There are times when we sense His delight and joy, when He seemingly is picking us up and tossing us about in the air like a small child in the hands of a parent in a park on a Thursday afternoon. And yet there are other times when, in our shame, disobedience, or pride, we work as hard as possible to be independent and away from God. Some days we feel more like a daughter or son of God than others. There are days when the presence is not just a fact, but a feeling.

Notice in the picture of the father and son, the father does most of the work. He is the one who brings the feeling of delight to the son by scooping him up in his arms. But notice the son was walking right next to the father. If the son had run off, or began disobeying his father by running in the street, would that moment have happened? It's hard to say. Our attentiveness to our heavenly Father and our obedience to Him will always set us up for moments of joy within His presence. But we have to be *with* Him in the deepest sense of the word—we must abide.

As I have spoken with hundreds of people through my pastoral ministry, I get the sense we have the wrong expectations of the God of the Bible. It can be easy to assume other people—even people in Scripture and influential people today—are constantly surrounded by God's peaceful presence. They are not. Even the more experienced Christians would say the *feeling* is certainly real, but it's not constant. We want to always *feel* close to Him instead of doing the hard work and remembering He's always near to us, trusting that the feeling of His weighty presence will come and go as we faithfully walk beside Him. What are the expectations we can have of the Father walking beside us?

TWO KINDS OF PRESENCE

The first thing to understand about God's presence is that it is multifaceted. That is, even as the Bible speaks about the presence of God, it speaks about it in many different ways. Theologians have divided these different ways by using the terms "general" and "manifest" nearness of God. Like the word "Trinity," the two terms do not appear directly in Scripture, but they help guide how Scripture talks about God's presence.

"General presence" refers to the truth that God is always present. Sometimes this is called His omnipresence. From Scripture we know that God is never completely absent from life. There is never a place God does not inhabit in some way (Ps. 72:19; 139; Isa. 6:3). As the psalmist says, "Where shall I go from your Spirit?" (139:7). There is nowhere we can go where God cannot. He, in some form, is generally present everywhere all of the time. Dallas Willard calls our planet a "God-Bathed World."[3]

Second, God has a "manifest presence." He shows up in a demonstrative and often dramatic way. He is somehow *more* present in one specific location with specific people. Most Old Testament accounts of our God surround some type of manifest-presence moment where there is thunder, fire, clouds of smoke, and/or loud noises (e.g., Ex. 19:19; 20:18; Ps. 18:8–13). In the New Testament we have records of moments like Jesus' baptism, the crucifixion/resurrection story, Pentecost, and certain conversion and preaching moments where God's presence is *manifested* among the people (Matt. 3:13–17; Mark 15:33, 16:11; Acts 2:1–4; 4:3). This is when we sense our heavenly Father's delight—the times when He scoops us up and throws us in the air.

These two kinds of presence relate to and play off each other. Both of them have a relationship to what we call God's *transcendence* and *immanence*. Transcendence is above and beyond us; God's immanence is more personal and intimate. The mysterious nature of God is that He is high and holy, but also near to us. Psalm 34 gives us a great picture of this mystery. It begins with a cry to "magnify" God and to lift up His name (vv. 1–3), but it closes by declaring that this same God is "near to the brokenhearted" and has turned "his ears toward their cry" (verses 18 and 15). God is both to be magnified—high and lifted up—and to be related with, because He is both *transcendent* and *immanent*.

RELATIONAL PRESENCE

So when we say, "I don't feel close to God right now," what are we talking about? Are we talking about the general presence or the manifest presence? While it might seem like we're clearly talking about the manifest presence, I want to make the case that we're actually talking about neither.

When we talk about God being "distant" from us, these two categories don't suffice. This is because we're talking about God's *relational* presence in our lives, the way we would talk about our wives, husbands, fathers, and mothers. This aspect of being *with God in relationship* is really what most of us mean when we talk about God's proximity.

As I grew up as a child, there was a sense in which my earthly father was always present with me. I share DNA with him, I am heavily influenced by his actions, and all of the money I ever carried or any resources I was afforded as a child were his. Beyond that, no matter where I went across my neighborhood, I was still his son—nothing could change that.

And still, when we would play basketball in the street or I would help him build something in the backyard, we would grow in our relationship and I would feel like *more of a son* to him when he came near physically. When his presence manifested itself in my life, I sensed joy and our relationship grew.

Our "relational presence" is our fellowship with God, our experience of Him in daily life, and what many Christians are thinking of when they tell people about God speaking to them. God, through His Holy Spirit, has a kind of presence that is relational. His Spirit is called "the Helper" (John 14:16) or "the Comforter" (KJV). Jesus instructs us to pray to "Our Father"(Matt. 6:9), and Paul tells us in Romans 8 how the Holy Spirit is to work in us in a personal, familial way when we think about God (vv. 12–17). The affectionate, personal language saturating the New Testament resonates with anyone who has felt close to God. This is how it should be.

THE DIFFERENCE BETWEEN OUR
LANGUAGE AND GOD'S STORY

There are not many places in Scripture where someone talks about God's presence the way many of us evangelicals talk about it. Throughout church history, many faithful followers have looked into the depths of this "presence." Very rarely do they speak about worship services like us or the "camp high." (For more on the "camp high" see the beginning of chapter 5.) In general, Christians speak about obeying God through prayer, Scripture reading, neighbor-loving, or social justice. We talk about it as we walk out of a touching worship service or after we hear a well-delivered message. Is this *really* God's presence we're talking about?

In American evangelicalism, we have created what Nichols has described as a "near-and-dear" type of God.[4] While we could possibly trace this type of thinking back through American evangelical faith, it seems nearly impossible to try and find the "near-and-dear" God in the Bible. If anything, the Bible gives us a picture of a God who is *terrifying* when His presence is manifested among human beings. Take nearly any biblical figure who met God and you will see a person collapse on the ground, overcome with fear and dread.

God is loving, gracious, and slow to anger, yes, but why do we assume we can handle all of that in perfect form all at once? The presence of God is not an easy place to stand, it appears. And yet, after these moments of intensity, there is a similar message given to Moses, David, Joseph, Peter, and many others after they fall on their face in fear: "Do not be afraid."

Despite these mighty pictures of God's presence, we are, at the same time, commanded by Scripture to seek His presence (Ps. 84:1–12; James 4:8). In the helpful academic book *The Presence of God*, J. Ryan Lister points out that God's mission across all of Scripture was to unite three things together: His *people*, in His *place*, with His *presence*.[5] We can see how this is certainly true all the way through creation, law, sacrifices, temples, priests, kings, prophets, exile, Messiah, the church, and even until Revelation. The end of the story of God is when these three things are united: God's people (the church), in God's place (the New Jerusalem), with God's presence (Father, Son, and Spirit). That's the story line of Scripture. God is high and holy, unlike us in nearly every way, and yet we, His creatures, are made for life with Him.

The terrifying, holy nature of God should not keep us from seeking His face and desiring His presence. Instead, when we look to Jesus, we see our invitation.

JESUS CHRIST AND THE GREAT PROMISE OF "IMMANUEL"

When Jesus Christ was born, the prophet Isaiah said one of His many names would be Immanuel, which literally means "God with us" (Isa. 7:14; Matt. 1:23). The startling message of the Gospels is not just, "God loves you," but "God has come to be with you." Remember the opening to the gospel of John? "The Word became flesh and dwelt among us" (John 1:14). Certain commentators conclude this line might as well be translated: "God came down and pitched his tent among us," referring to the Old Testament tabernacle, which was a sort of portable temple where God would dwell. Jesus came to begin the process of dwelling with His people (fulfilling the prayer of Solomon in 1 Kings 8:27–30). Through His life, death, and resurrection, we now obtain life in His name. By the coming of Jesus, history and the way humans relate to God has changed forever.

Jesus' primary message announced "the good news of the kingdom of God" (Luke 8:1). The news to us remains: God has made a way, and He is now accessible through the life and work of Christ. This is why He came, proclaiming the good news to those who are mourning, spiritually bankrupt, sick, and enslaved—they are no longer outside of God's space, His kingdom. Now, as we believe in Jesus, the fullness of God is made manifest in the power of God's Holy Spirit. We become God's temple, the storehouse and dwelling place of the Almighty Himself.

As followers of Christ, we have the Holy Spirit now dwelling in us—both corporately as the church and individually as believers (John 14:15–31; Acts 1:8; Rom. 8:1–11; 1 Cor. 3:16–17). Jesus gives us the Holy Spirit so God can dwell now with men and women in order to change them and empower them to do God's will on earth as it's done in heaven. This is not just a feeling; this is a fact for believers.

> Jesus gives us the Holy Spirit in order to change men and women and empower them to do God's will on earth.

The beauty of Jesus is in the incarnation—the transcendent God has come to be permanently immanent—God with us, our "Immanuel" (Matt. 1:23)—through the work of His Son Jesus and the Holy Spirit (John 1:14, Matt. 28:19–20). The name of Jesus always means good news, and as we work to know where God resides in our lives, we must continually look back to Him as the fulfillment of "Immanuel," God with us.

TWO KEY QUESTIONS

As we see the truth of Scripture, questions still remain. Two key questions arise since many of us still feel distant from God, even though we have the Holy Spirit within us through the history-altering work of Jesus Christ. We wonder why God does not always feel near to us.

The first question we have to ask ourselves is a very difficult question, but an essential one. You and I have to ask, *Are we actually filled with God's Holy Spirit?* The apostle Paul commands us to let the Holy Spirit fill and control us (Eph. 5:18). It's very easy for us to simply say we're a Christian, attend church, and say all of the right things. It's a very different thing to be empowered by the Holy Spirit—to have God, who lives inside us (Rom. 5:5; 1 Cor. 6:19), controlling us. Don't answer this question lightly, but study Scripture and ask yourself if you are really filled with the Spirit—and ask the Spirit of God to fill you each day.

If you need help knowing if you are or are not filled with the Spirit, a simple look at Galatians 5:16–26 is helpful. By walking in the power of the Spirit, you will have love, joy, peace, patience, kindness, etc., growing in your life. Do you have these fruits (vv. 22–23), and are they increasing? Additionally, how have you been changing? Do you sense new desires forming in your life to obey God and learn more about Him? Are you convicted of your selfishness and pride regularly? Do you desire wrongdoing and impurity to be out of your life entirely? The sign of the Spirit in a person's life is the transformation of their character.

The second key question, if you believe yourself to be filled with the Spirit, is, *Are we paying attention to the work and presence of the Holy Spirit in our life?* The Holy Spirit is not a thing; the Holy Spirit is a person. And just like any person or relationship, we must pay attention to the Spirit. He is our guide and our closest ally within our hidden life in Christ, but we cannot expect Him to be constantly badgering us. We must turn our heart, mind, and soul in His direction. We must ask what we do to receive the gift of His constant presence.

PRACTICING AND TRUSTING
THE PRESENCE OF GOD

There may not be a more famous writer on the subject of God's presence than Brother Lawrence. The funny thing about Brother Lawrence is that he didn't write down most of his thoughts on God. In the little book, *The Practice of the Presence of God*, Brother Lawrence's wisdom was written down over three hundred years ago, partially by him and partially by his close friend and abbot, Joseph de Beaufort.[6]

Lawrence was a simple cook and a servant. He was not a scholar or a leader in the church. In fact, legend has it that Brother Lawrence was not accepted by the monastery or the army, and so he decided to cook and serve. However, people would travel miles to hear from him because his wisdom and presence were so powerful. Brother Lawrence became a master of relating to God on a daily basis through ordinary practice and service, and his little book continues to sell thousands of copies.

"The presence of God," he writes in a letter to a friend, "is the concentration of the soul's attention on God, remembering he is always present."[7] To Brother Lawrence and mystic Christians like him across many traditions, God's presence was not always something *He withdraws*, but something *we withdraw from*. God's nearness is mostly about our recognizing that God is always near through His Spirit. To take from the story at the beginning of this chapter—where we watch a young father in a park scoop up his small son in his arms—if we are not walking alongside the Father, we will not be available to be swept up in His arms.

At the same time, Psalms 13 and 42 would communicate there are simply times God goes away. For one reason or another, our *relational* proximity with God changes. God's presence is still with us in the *factual* sense—we know God is with us because Jesus promised this to us—but we lack the relational closeness. Much like the analogy with my wife: she may be in the house and still legally my wife, but sometimes the relational proximity is lacking due to my lesser attention to her or my greater attention to my decisions.

Our lack of attentiveness to God's presence and work is

what primarily brings us further away from Him. This is how we stop walking by His side as His sons and daughters. Our drifting happens because we stop looking at the shore. And so we can now see how the story of Adam and Eve repeats itself: when we gratify our sin, we go into hiding, but God seeks us all the more. He comes after us in our sin, but we do not always want to be found. Instead, we want to cover ourselves up, shirk responsibility, and act like everything will be fine at some point. *We* are the issue. As Christians, we have lost our identity as sons and daughters, and we stand outside of God's house, making every excuse we can think about to not go inside and join the party we convince ourselves isn't that great anyways.

God is always with us, and everything He has is available to us. We are the ones who have not utilized His heavenly resources. We become lazy, distracted, and enslaved to the many selfish decisions we make over and over again, instead of taking advantage of all He has given us. We stop looking for Him in the people we serve at work, we stop praying for our classmates and co-workers, we lose our imagination in our churches, and we just . . . drift.

> When we gratify our sin, we go into hiding, but God seeks us all the more. He comes after us in our sin.

If being near to God is about paying attention to God's nearness to us, then we have work to do.

And yet, we must be careful. God's presence is not something we dictate, but something God blesses us with. I cannot continue writing without warning you: this book is not a step-by-step manual. We cannot manipulate God by doing particular religious acts in order to summon Him. He is no genie; rather, He is the Almighty God who has come near to us in Jesus Christ and can bless us with an overwhelming sense that He is near.

We need to find this balance and walk the tightrope of God's presence by making ourselves always available, always aware of this Immanuel God. As Brother Lawrence said, we must "direct our soul's attention" to Him. It will then be in His power to pour His blessed presence on us. We must focus on walking alongside our Father, trusting He will give us an experience of intimacy with Him as He sees necessary.

LEARNING TO PRACTICE

For the most part, I do what my wife asks me to do. While you could certainly psychoanalyze me or make a solid case that I'm simply afraid of her, the truth is I do what Ali asks because I love her and I want to please her. If she asks me to unload the dishwasher, clean the bathroom, pick up groceries as I'm coming home from work, I will make sure I do those things in a timely manner simply for the reason that Ali is my wife and I love her.

But let's say I just stopped doing what Ali asks me to do. Maybe, one rainy Saturday I'm watching college basketball on our couch when she asks me if I could walk our dog. Let's—for the sake of example—say that from that day forward I never said "yes" to anything she asked of me for the next three months. Do you think that would affect our relationship?

If you answer that question in any way other than "absolutely," you are probably not married. The reality of our relationships is simple: our actions *toward* others are tied to our intimacy *with* others.

Do you believe that your pride affects your relationship with God? In the emphasis on preaching on forgiveness over the past fifty years of evangelicalism, pastors have lost the essential teaching on holiness. We have become like the ungrateful servant of Matthew 18, whose debt was graciously forgiven all while his heart remained hardened, greedy, and unchanged (vv. 21–35). God's response to such a person is not to be underestimated. The decisions we make change our proximity with God. Our actions *toward* God are tied to our intimacy *with* God.

I am surprised at how many people are caught off guard when I ask them questions surrounding this. When they come to talk with me about the distance between God and them, they do not expect me to ask them about their regular life. When people come to a pastor, they expect prayer, Scripture, and churchy things. But often when someone speaks to me about feeling distant from God I ask the person a simple question: "When was the last time you did something, and the only reason you did it was because God asked you to?" Sometimes, when I'm speaking with young students, I'll start by simply asking them about their relationship with their parents. Are you honoring them? How's life at home? Have you been dishonest with someone close to you? Are there certain behaviors

Our actions *toward* God are tied to our intimacy *with* God.

you are hiding from all of your relationships? These are all things that I believe are wrapped up in our experience of God and His presence.

Sin—in its various forms and descriptions—hurts our relationship with God. Many of us have felt what Paul told the Corinthian believers about sexual sin: "Do you not know that your bodies are members of Christ? Shall I then take the members of Christ and make them members of a prostitute? Never!" Later he added, "Or do you not know that your body is a temple of the Holy Spirit within you, whom you have from God? You are not your own, for you were bought with a price. So glorify God in your body" (1 Cor. 6:15, 19–20). What we do with our bodies affects how we relate with God.

Or what about when Peter warned husbands to "live with your wives in an understanding way . . . so that your prayers may not be hindered" (1 Peter 3:7)? Paul summarized some of this thinking to the Roman church by saying, "Do you not know that if you present yourselves to anyone as obedient slaves, you are slaves of the one whom you obey, either of sin, which leads to death, or of obedience, which leads to righteousness?" (Rom. 6:16).

We need to catch this: our daily decisions will affect our experience of God's presence, both negatively and positively. Look again at those verses from 1 Corinthians, 1 Peter, and Romans: how we live with our spouses will affect our prayers, and our choices with our bodies play with our relationship with the Holy Spirit. Our actions and God's presence are not two separate things—they are deeply connected. We cannot afford to live any longer under the lie that our decisions do not matter. If we are not walking beside the Father, the chances of Him scooping us up in His arms become less likely. We'll look at this more in the next section, but it's important for us to begin thinking about this as we get a sense for what our expectations are for God and His presence.

While our sin affects His presence negatively, our obedience lends us to be available to Him all the more. This is what this book is for: to remind us of the beauty and reality of God's presence and to show us again what we can do to be available to receive it.

THE FEELING

I've been dating my wife for over ten years. You can imagine, between our dating life and our married life together, our feelings toward each another have not stayed stagnant. Unfortunately, there are moments in marriage where you feel angry and distant from your spouse. By God's grace, my wife and I do not have many moments like this, but they exist. There are also seasons where married couples are not angry but things just feel distant. Through heavy work seasons or times of stress, it is not uncommon for me to feel far from my wife.

Still, healthy married people will tell you there are also remarkable moments in marriage. There are times when, seemingly out of nowhere, your eyes meet and you remember how deeply grateful you are for that person. It surprises you, but you'll be driving together or walking the dog or doing some simple chore around the house and catch their eye, seeing in them not just the moment, but the many moments you have shared, as if all of those many moments suddenly crashed into this one and you gush, "I love you."

As I have reflected on this, I realize that these moments come out only in healthy relationships. The more I am forgiving toward my wife and helpful to her, and encouraging to her, praying for her, etc., the more opportunity I give myself to *feel* the loving relationship I have with my wife. But if I am proud, bitter, and begrudging toward Ali and constantly ignoring her needs, not listening to her voice, I cannot expect the feeling of love to follow.

With God, the feeling of His nearness is similar: *it comes from somewhere*. The feeling comes after seasons of obeying His Word, resisting temptation, ambitiously praying, and thoughtfully responding to His Holy Spirit's direction. The feeling comes after a season of a lack of feeling. The intensity and joyful experience come from a decent time of ordinary faithfulness where you are simply trying to please God, and that joy surprises you.

I think a lot of us seek a feeling of God instead of God Himself. Have you noticed after a worship service how we will say things like, "Worship was so good!" What does that mean? Normally, we mean we experienced something great during the music. But worship is not about us; worship is about God. How quickly we make something meant for Him about us. I'm afraid we worship sensation more than God Himself.

God's presence is available to us; we need not rely on

feeling it, but knowing it because we know *Him*. And yes, we may, through inspired lyrics or the power of the Scriptures, even know Him better during a worship service. Our desire should always be to know Him better. The feeling will surprise you—it will come and go. Remember, God is the goal, the prize, and the One. The feeling is the extra blessing. It will come at times, and we will feel the joy of being swept up in His arms, but focusing on it is the wrong way to receive it. That's how relationships work.

> God is the goal, the prize, and the One. The feeling is the extra blessing.

HIDDEN

Throughout church history and the Christian tradition, those desiring to meet with God directly in His presence have been called "mystics." Thomas Aquinas, Dionysius, and John Bonaventure are among the more famous in the crowd. I've never been a big fan of this word—"mystic"—because it makes the seeking of God's presence seem like an odd sect where only *some* Christians belong. My ministry life would testify toward the opposite. Most of the people I interact with desire to meet with God. They also have a profound conviction that they should be able to.

Nevertheless, the term "mystic" literally means, "hidden." The men and women of this tradition knew God was present; they were convinced He was in their midst, but also needing to be found. They saw "the world" as a place covering up the goodness of God and the presence of His Holy Spirit. They are the ones who trained themselves and us to see through the world we constructed—a world filled with shopping carts, twenty-four-hour news programs, and bleary eyes set before screens. We must go to school as the mystics did—searching for the hiddenness of the God who sits in plain sight.

The mystics are famous for the visions they saw and the experiences they had—some shocking and more bizarre than anything you'll see on the Internet. However, when I began to read more about the mystics, I was surprised to learn they also led very normal lives, keeping their hands busy with menial work like farming, book-binding, and wine-making. They also kept tight schedules. They started before the sun rose and were in bed before it fully set, filling most of their days with three things: prayer, work, and meditation.

What is most surprising about discovering the hidden beauty of God's presence is that it includes our participation and work. But we need not delve into trippy, overly spiritual conquests. Rather, we must do what the mystics did: find God on earth. We know we will find Him in heaven, but for now, as we realize the distance between us and the sin that can wreck this intimacy, we must learn the hard work of seeking God's presence. We need to close the distance and to find what is hidden, but has been there all along.

Part 2

CLOSING THE DISTANCE

I AM SITTING on the large green chair in our home office, staring out the window and drinking a glass of water when my sister-in-law, Libby, peeks in her head. She's been living with us, and I have just returned from a weeklong middle school camp I helped lead. My exhaustion is just beginning to set in.

"Welcome home," Libby says.

"Yeah, good to be back," I offer.

"Did Ali tell you about her rough week?" Libby asks.

Through my week away, I hadn't spoken to Ali much because cell service and Internet were limited where I was staying. "No . . . what happened?"

Libby and Ali are close sisters, and her face changes as she tells me about the week I didn't know my wife had. Ali was starting her fourth and final year as a medical student, just nine months shy of becoming a doctor, when she spent five weeks with the pediatric intensive care unit. This is where the sickest and more difficult cases come and, because it is a pediatric floor, every room has someone under eighteen. Needless to say, this is a difficult place sometimes.

My wife's week while I was gone was painful, heartbreaking, and special all at once. On top of a tough week, her rotation as a medical student required her to work eighty hours in just one week, including one "overnight" shift that lasted thirty straight hours! This was her regular schedule for over a month. My exhaustion suddenly felt insignificant.

As Libby talked, I began feeling sad and far away from Ali. She wasn't home yet and I began to miss her, wishing she could be with me so I could give her a hug and encourage her. The thought came into my head: *the only way I can feel close to her is if I do something for her.* But with her not being physically present, my options were limited.

"Looks like we need flowers and chocolate," I tell Libby.

"I was thinking the same thing."

My weariness fades into a healthy adrenaline as I grab my car keys from the dining room table and head for the car and to the market. There I select a large bouquet and some fancy chocolate. My confidence boosts and I suddenly feel connected to my wife. Back home, I pace a little in my room anxiously awaiting her arrival, anticipating our time together when I could see her respond to a simple act of love. A realization suddenly hits me: without seeing her, my action *toward* Ali has built intimacy *with* Ali.

The sound of her car reaches the driveway and the door opens.

Chapter 5

ABIDING/OBEYING

**Closeness to God isn't about feelings;
closeness to God is about obedience.**[1]
RICH MULLINS

You don't need to be in youth ministry for very long to learn its vernacular. One term in particular will show up in your first few weeks: the "camp high."

The camp high is simple. A student goes to summer camp or a missions trip, and for that one week, they feel as if they are on a mountaintop, always sensing God's presence and feeling closer to Him than ever before. But, as the phrase entails, it is just a "high." And, even though we are Christians and would never do drugs, we know enough about a high to know it does not last. As school starts and schedules change, the camp high fades away and we must survive another nine months before we really sense God's presence again.

By this unfortunate logic, our relationship with God is predicated upon a particular experience or place. Many of my students desire to go back to camp and work there for a long period of time, or return to a missions location because that's where they sensed God. But this can be unhealthy. If you can only experience and grow in Christ in one particular place and with limited temptations or real-life experiences, how will you live life in the dangerous world surrounding us? We need Christians who are able to sustain their joy for Jesus in the marketplace, universities, and creative centers of the world. Jesus has not saved us *from* the world, but *to it,* for its redemption. We cannot live in such a way where our relationship with God is stabilized by a particular type of experience. If it is, then we will seek such an experience, and not Him.

Surprisingly, the only other time (other than the "camp high") that I consistently hear of people being near to God is during intense suffering. I know suffering has the ability to do the opposite, but I've been shocked at how many people *find* God in the darkness of life instead of miss Him. I can relate and perhaps you can too. As Keller says, "You don't realize Jesus is all you need until Jesus is all you have." Often, at the very bottom of everything, there is a beautiful communion to be had with Christ. Paul calls this "sharing in the sufferings of Christ." Suffering strips us of all of the things we think make us happy and, after those things are all gone, we find out we never needed any of it. We just need Him.

BETWEEN THE HIGHS AND THE LOWS

We need some middle ground. As I said earlier, we need some help with the long plains of faith. Yes, God seems to be with us when things go south and everything is taken away, or when we are at camp or in a powerful church service and life is going super well. It is in the middle ground, however—the ordinary and regular—when God seems distant . . . or not there at all. It's when we're two months into school, or deep in the days of winter, after ten hours into a draining work shift, that God is nowhere to be found and we get somewhat upset at the lack of God's showing up in our life.

We need help with the everyday and the ordinary because it seems like during the extraordinary we know a bit more about where God is. But the problem is that we spend most of our days doing the ordinary stuff of life. Laundry must be done, papers have due dates, and shifts need to be worked.

It all raises the question: *can we experience God and His presence in everyday life, or are we doomed to feel at a distance?*

We have every right to be frustrated with the everydayness of finding God. Between the daily routines and the recurring deadlines, our desire for the presence of God can get lost. The answer is, we must recognize that our desire for His presence is a gift from God Himself that we must seek.

Before I became a Christian, I did not desire God's presence; I actually tried to avoid it. I can remember growing up in Catholic school, dreading the thought of mass some weeks because I didn't want to face God and all of the imagery that goes with the service—the bread, wine, incense, etc. I did not want to sense God's Spirit because I knew I was no good and had been ignoring Him. It was like that

Life not only *can* be lived with God, but it *must* be lived with God.

awkward moment when you forget to text someone back and then you see them in person. I didn't want to have to explain myself. But now, because of God's work in my life, I desire to have the Holy Spirit active in my life, and when I do not *feel* Him, I also get upset. Part of the change is my understanding that life not only *can* be lived with God, but it *must* be lived with God.

God's presence and our relationship to it must be thought about with care, because we cannot keep counting on experiences or some type of suffering to fuel us every year. Even worse, we cannot wish for suffering to enter into our lives just so we can "feel" near to God. This is not the way Jesus lived and it is not the way the church fathers seemed to think about things. There must be a way to know that God is near whether we are suffering, thrilled, or somewhere in the commonplace of life, emptying the dishwasher or driving home from work.

Connecting with God in the ordinary stuff of life is more difficult and takes more effort on our part. But luckily we have the Master Teacher to listen to on the subject.

ABIDING IN THE FATHER

Jesus Christ lived, as Robert E. Coleman says, "in total dependence" and "oneness with the Father" all of His days on earth.[3] Is this not what we desire—to live in "oneness" with the divine? Jesus was never far from His Father and considered His connection to the Trinity of first importance. Beyond this, Jesus' work is constantly being mentioned as "in the power of the Holy Spirit," meaning He was relying on the power of the triune God to propel His ministry and sustain His life.

We often do not consider, however, *why* Jesus was close to God. So often, we chalk it up to the fact that "He was Jesus," a lazy intellectual jump that lands us in a place of shortly sustained peace. Was Jesus close to God just because He was God or for another reason? I believe Scripture would say that there is another reason.

In His humanity, Jesus laid down His rights as God, deciding to make Himself nothing (Phil. 2:6–11). This is why, when Jesus was tempted to play His "God card"—whether it be by calling a legion of angels to save Him on the cross or to gain all the earthly kingdoms of the world in a deal with the devil—He never took advantage of it. Jesus was *decidedly* human while in His nature fully God.

Could it be that Jesus was close to His Father for a different reason?

In all of our lazy hermeneutics, we've forgotten a key piece as to why He was so near to His Father. Jesus of Nazareth was near to His Father because He obeyed His Father perfectly. Jesus' entire life was placed under submission to His Father's mission for Him. He says it all of the time: I only do what My Father in heaven asks of Me.[4] Jesus' nearness to God was connected to obedience. He prayed, meditated day and night, paid attention to the needs of others, and sought the Father's will in every situation. All of these decisions were decisions of perfect obedience (John 5:19–47).

It makes sense, then, that Jesus would teach His followers

to immerse themselves in the same reality (or, "baptize . . . in the name of the Father, the Son, and the Holy Spirit [Matt. 28:19]). His final words instructed the disciples to do so. He said, "Teach them to obey," a powerful closing command from our Master. He understood that the most important thing we could do with our lives is not tell people to agree with us about Jesus, but show people how obedience to God can result in a life that flourishes in His presence.

In John 15, Jesus describes how we will be invited into this divine dance between Himself and the triune God. We will not be left out to dry, but rather brought in on this remarkable, eternal relationship. Jesus' invitation is for us to *"abide"* in Him. He promises that if we do this, we will not only survive, but thrive by "bearing much fruit." He gives us the simple analogy of a vine and its branches—this is how interconnected we are to be with God. We are completely connected to God as we abide in Jesus Christ. This all sounds lovely in theory, but if you're like me, there are many questions circling, and the first is simple: "How does one abide?" In His wisdom, Jesus tells us clearly: "If you keep my commandments, you *will* abide in my love" (John 15:10, emphasis added).

A simple equation, perhaps: obeying = abiding.

Why is this important?

OBEDIENCE LEADS TO ABIDING IN GOD

During my times of pastoral counseling, I cannot place much confidence in changing a person's feelings. If the individual comes feeling far from God, it is difficult to spend an hour with that person and *give* them the feeling of the presence of God as they leave. I'm no magician. However, what I have come to understand is this: God's presence in our life results in certain feelings at certain times, but not *all* of the time. In fact, it's rare that people in the Bible talk like we talk. Have you noticed this? There are very few places where people speak of *feeling* God is near, but there are a lot of places where writers speak of *knowing* God is near.

Have you considered the difference? It's true: God has varying degrees of presence. We already talked about God having "manifest" presence where an inordinate amount of God is in a particular place. But then there's also God's general presence—His omnipresence—and also the presence of the Holy Spirit in the life of all believers that no matter what we do, we cannot change. There are different variations on how God shows up in our lives, and this "abiding" is one way we know God is near.

The word "abide" is a word of peace and assurance, of resting and relaxing. We need to reclaim this word in our faith. Our lives are filled with the smallest anxieties, only increased as our phones sit ready to buzz in our pockets, delivering us news of attention, sadness, joy, stress, and every other emotion on the planet. We do not need more people concerned about how they are perceived or what will happen to them. We worry plenty. We need to learn how to abide.

Jesus speaks of this "abiding" as a special type of presence in the life of the believer that seems to rest on those who simply do what He has asked. Therefore, the key question to me is not, *"Do I feel God's presence?"* but

> If you are doing what Jesus asks of you, you are with Him, abiding and in fellowship with Him.

rather, *"Am I doing what Jesus has asked me to do?"* If you are doing what Jesus asks of you, you are with Him, abiding and in fellowship with Him, and you can trust the feeling or sense of His presence to come as He allows. This is His promise to you. We need to be reminding ourselves of the importance of obedience, of taking what He has asked of us and actually *practicing* it—no matter how clunky it may be.

Think about the example I've used before with the child and his father. In order for the child to experience the joy of the father's presence, wouldn't it only help if the child carefully did whatever his father told him to do? If the little child runs into the street and screams, he will still be the child and the father would still love him, but wouldn't it strain the relationship and change the *kind* of presence the father has? Maybe it would change the afternoon.

Obedience does not *make us sons or daughters of God—* only Christ can and has done that for us. Instead, obedience securely places us within the relational presence of God. We have more opportunities to sense God's presence when we are faithfully walking next to Him. This is Jesus' image of "abiding." It comes through our loving and grateful obedience.

WHO IS WORTH TRUSTING TO FULLY OBEY?

While not a perfect metaphor, I think it helps me understand God and me. When I do things *for* God and obey His commands and take His teachings seriously, it shows both Him and me that I have great love for Him. My actions *toward and for* God build intimacy *with* God. Where there is obedience, there is a strange and comforting rest that occurs as well. Sure, this metaphor breaks down, but that's because no person (my wife included) can be trusted with all-out obedience *except* God Himself—and He is entirely worth it.

When we think of obeying parents and obeying teachers, we do not exactly attach the word "happiness" or "enjoyment" to it. But what if you were obeying the Author of Life? What if you changed the source of your obeying? What if you began to listen to the smartest Man who has ever lived—the one who lived a perfect life and has instructed us on how to replicate it? The words of Jesus in the Bible offer such instructions.

Jesus' teachings, as He declared, are a light load, and they are not complicated (Matt. 11:28–30). He tells you to practice life without anger, because it is better that way. He recognizes that a grudge is easy to hold, but forgiveness is better. He instructs us to delete lust in our lives so we might not betray vows we make to our spouse. Our "yes" should stay that way, and we should not be mixed up in lying or in saying we will do something and then not following through with it. He tells you to give to all of the people in your life who beg and that giving is better than receiving. He tells you to pray and to do so privately. And so many more commands that you should continue to read and practice.

This is life with Jesus. We follow Him because He is

right about everything and all His ways are good and all those ways lead us down a path of a joyful life—or what He called "the abundant life."

This is why, after all of this talk about abiding and obeying in John 15, Jesus says this: "These things I have spoken to you, that my joy may be in you, and that your joy may be full" (John 15:11).

Obedience is not something we do because we have to; it is something we do in order that we may receive Jesus' joy. Jesus was a joyful man and it is obvious through a brief reading of His life that attaining such joy is not an easy thing. Even though He experienced a vast array of emotions, experiences, and circumstances, Jesus maintained His joy. Hebrews says that even through the cross he had a "joy that was set before him" (Heb. 12:1–2). This is why followers of His through the centuries have been able to sit in jail cells and on trial for death and maintain a level of peace and comfort. Paul calls this "the secret" to being able to rejoice in all circumstances (Phil. 4:12). We all want to be joyful, but we are scared of what it may take.

> Obedience is not something we do because we have to; we do it that we may receive Jesus' joy.

The beauty of following Jesus' commands is that there will never be a time in your life where you can't do it. As you read the testimonies of Scripture and stories of church fathers and courageous missionaries through the ages, it is clear to me that it is always possible to practice what Jesus is asking you to do. You can be in prison or walking through your own neighborhood, you can be facing execution or facing your teenager—there will never be a time in your life where you cannot obey Jesus. By His grace, you always can, and you always should, because only in obeying Him might we abide in an "inexpressible joy."

This kind of obedience leaves us available to the healing, peaceful, and real presence of God. "Through the ages," Dallas Willard writes, "the sustaining power of the Beloved Presence has made the sickbed sweet and the graveside triumphant . . . [and] brought glory to drudgery, poverty and old age."[5]

I desire this presence, and I know you do too. My desire, however, is to find it even when circumstances are not so extreme. I desire to live my life within this presence, even if it means I cannot always sense it and feel it.

WHAT IS IT ABOUT THE "CAMP HIGH"?

For students in our church (and yours too), camp highs don't happen just on camping retreats. Feeling close to God also happens on missions trips. Each year, when our students travel on our annual missions trips, I tell them precisely why they are currently feeling close to God. For the first time in their life, they have laid down everything for the sake of following Jesus Christ. They do not have their phones, they sever dating relationships, they're unconcerned with money and appearance, they pray and read Scripture daily, and they dedicate themselves to the needs of others. It should not be a shock that upon consecrating themselves in such a way, they would sense anew the presence of God in their life.

As I tell them this, I ask this question: "Why can't you do what you did this week at home?" The reality is, we have not done anything on a missions trip that a student cannot do at home. To be sure, the particulars will change and the people and locations will be different, but why can we not go home and dedicate the *next* week to meeting the needs of others and seeking the presence and leading of the Holy Spirit? When you take a week to rearrange your priorities and make your service to God and others first, it's no wonder God seems so near to you . . . you are doing the very thing He has asked you to do.

In a brief interview online, one prominent scholar of early Christian mysticism, Bernard McGinn, says that not all Christians will experience wild visions (or, to put it in modern, youth group terms, "a camp high"), but rather, "often [Christians receive] a very, very deep sense of God's presence in their lives that transforms them . . . changes them. . . . The test is love of God and love of neighbor. And as that gets deeper and deeper and deeper, that's the sign that God is really present."[6]

Jesus said, "Whoever has my commandments and keeps them . . . I will love him and manifest myself to him" (John 14:21). The more we practice these commands and see them in our lives, the more God is with us in the deepest sense and He will manifest Himself to us. We cannot expect God's presence to crash into our lives out of nowhere because, remember, *it comes from somewhere*.

We need to focus on Jesus' commandments, then. What is it that we are doing when God is near, and how can we cultivate those actions in our daily lives? Who are the great ones in faith and what did they do that we are not doing? And how might we change what we're doing? By obeying the ways of God, we *will* abide in Him—there is no question—Jesus has promised us this.

God is the *living* God, and I believe so many of us walk through our lives missing the greatest resource available to us—Him. We busy ourselves making appointments, scrolling through our phones, and watching endless amounts of the lives of other people on television when the Almighty God is hovering through the earth, searching and beckoning for those who might desire to be connected to Him and hidden with Him.

In the following chapters, I want to examine the things students of Jesus have done for centuries and the things Jesus Himself did. When Jesus says, "If you obey my commands," what are those commands He is speaking of? What are the things that, if we practice them, could bring us close to Him? As we look at them, it would serve us well to start in some small way to practice these things not so that God would love *us*, but so that we might actually show we love *Him*. In this way, our actions *toward* Him will build intimacy *with* Him.

Chapter 6

PRAYING/LISTENING

Prayer is laborious (active) when a man's heart is far away from him and God is far from the heart.[1]

ST. GREGORY

When I was eighteen my parents drove me to Seattle, where I would start my first year of college. I was allowed into my dorm room two full weeks before my roommate because I had been hired on campus to flip burgers and make fries in the cafeteria (it was just as bad as you think). My early move-in date allowed me to pick the more comfortable bed, take the best desk, and find the perfect spot for the mini fridge I won during my high school graduation all-nighter that past June.

There's this sweet spot in between graduation and your freshman year where there really is no reality—you live in a world of dreams. Your high school years are far behind and the memories begin being edited in your mind—even if you've made half of them up or left them grossly exaggerated. And the frustrations and mistakes of college or young adulthood haven't happened yet, and so you exist within a belief that you'll make all of the right choices and great things will happen to you (this is also how you spend a lot of your twenties).

I remember thinking how dominant my Hacky Sack abilities would be, or how I would learn every Dave Matthews Band song on guitar, or how I would captain an Ultimate Frisbee team or a sensational intramural basketball squad (none of these things came to pass).

The fog of this unreality is fun for a summer, but it doesn't last when you have grades to make up and friendships to repair and an academic major to figure out. Work needs to get done and you've got to figure out how to do it.

My mom and dad moved me in and made sure everything was in its right place. Mom did her mom thing of making certain the bedding was all there while my dad fiddled with the television I had bought a month earlier. My RA came by, said hello to the folks, told me he was excited to get to know me, made a joke, and was on his way to other early arrival students. After the bedding was put together and the TV was all set up, my parents looked awkwardly at each other and then back to me.

"Well . . . " my mom said with some desperation, as if to think of another thing that could keep them around another minute.

"Yeah . . ." offered my dad.

Neither of them wanted to be the first one to say goodbye, and so I decided to take the hit.

"I'll see you around Thanksgiving . . . it's not that big of a deal," I told them.

After some hugs, my mom cried a little bit and we all said goodbye. My parents walked out of the dorm floor and closed the door behind them, leaving me with the silence of a half-empty dorm floor. For just a second, I was sad. This sadness led me to do what most Americans do when they're sad: turn on the television. I will never forget this moment when I turned on the TV to see the Dallas Cowboys playing the New York Giants. I do not remember this moment because it was a particularly special game; I remember this moment because this was when a wave of understanding and ecstasy hit my mind. Suddenly, amidst the noise of the game and the sadness of seeing my parents go, I realized I could do whatever I wanted, whenever I wanted, all of the time. No longer could my mom tell me to unload the dishwasher because *there was no dishwasher*. I would never be told to eat dinner *because dinner was now available at 1 a.m.* No more mom to ask me "how my day was" after school *because there would be no conversations after school.* This freedom hit me so tangibly I think I may have giggled.

Free. Now. Forever.

Well, sort of. Anyone who has gone to college understands the "freedom" we experience can lead to all sorts of disasters like missing exams, poor diet, and wasting massive amounts of time and money all at once. The transition to college freedom includes a learning curve. This learning curve happened to me when my mom called me forty-seven hours after she had left me in that dorm room alone watching the Dallas Cowboys play the New York Giants.

"Honey?"

"Yeah, Mom?"

"Everything OK?"

"Yeah, everything's fine. Why?"

"I just haven't heard from you is all and I got a bit worried."

"It's been two days," I said.

During those first weeks I wondered why I should call my parents ever again. I wanted to be free, to do *my thing* and to catch up with them later during Christmas break or next summer when I would impress them with all of my cool stories about my Frisbee team.

But the problem is that relationships don't work this way. Relationships don't exist *for us* to feel awesome; relationships exist for us to learn how to sacrifice and make others feel awesome. Our even deeper problem is that most of us get into relationships to feel awesome as opposed to learning the art of generous living. We date to make out, not to pay for dinner. We get married for "happiness" instead of to be taught humility, faithfulness, and holiness. Our love for having people think we're awesome seems to trump our desire to give for the sake of other people's joy.

And doesn't this translate to our relationship with God? I think I first started following God because He made me feel good about myself, but that's no reason to *keep* following Him. The more we spend time with God we realize *He* is awesome and we are far from it.

Imagine if, after my parents had left me at college and I turned off the Cowboys game, I locked the door, changed my phone number, and never responded to emails, social media messages, or letters. Imagine if the only time I reached out to them was for the one thing a college student *really needs:* money. What if I had stopped talking to them entirely? Would that change our relationship?

Duh.

Another example: if I told you I loved my wife and you asked me, "When was the last time you talked to her?" and I said, "Six weeks ago," would you still think I loved her?

Every relationship you've ever sustained over a long period of time included, without fail, good, consistent communication. Relationships starve when communication ceases. No communication means no relationship.

And so, might I ask why we think it's any different with God?

THE GIFT OF PRAYER

God has given us a way to communicate with Him called prayer. And while we may think we know most of what prayer is all about, it is important to think through this ancient, mysterious art of talking to God and listening for Him. As we talk about God's presence and our proximity to Him, there's no way of avoiding our communication issue.

Have you ever stopped and thought about this—just the *idea* of prayer? Prayer happens when a human talks to God and when God speaks to a human being. We humans have access and ability to communicate with the infinite, magnificent, glorious, Divine Being in heaven who created us. We can talk to God. Without doing a particular religious ritual or reciting specific words, we are free to call out to the one who made mountains, hearts, and heaven.

Upon our redemption through belief in Jesus as Savior, this communication forms the foundation of our relationship with the Father. As I wrote in chapter 5 about obedience being the key to abiding in Jesus, prayer becomes our first point of reference as to what Christians should actually be obeying.

Some of us haven't thought through our prayer life in weeks. This gift of prayer is remarkable and I wonder if we simply need the reminder to use its wonder. When we stop talking to our friends, our friendships fail, and when we stop talking with God, our relationship with Him fails too. It is a gift to communicate—and God has allowed us to communicate with Him, so let's use this gift of prayer.

After nearly ten years in youth ministry, I have to confess I grew a bit tired of hearing certain answers after particular questions. I can't tell you how many times I sat around a small group where the "application" from our lesson together was to "read the Bible daily and pray more."

One morning I asked a discipleship group of senior guys a question and then added: "And don't say 'read your Bible and pray more' because I'm tired of that answer." They all kind of looked at me funny as if to say, "Well, what else is there?"

When I drove home after our small group, I thought about their faces looking back at me like I was crazy. Was I crazy? I began thinking about how much a devotional life of reading my Bible daily and praying more has truly shaped my life—it has changed me and increased my love for God over time. Scripture reading and prayer may be the most important spiritual disciplines we will do to remind us of God's constant presence in our lives.

So today I tend to think differently. Now I realize that if we would really read our Bibles every day and pray multiple times a day—whether we felt like it or not—our love for God would grow and our awareness of His presence would infiltrate our minds and hearts. We would be transformed.

> Scripture reading and prayer may be the most important spiritual disciplines to remind us of God's constant presence.

We have this gift of actually speaking to our Creator and listening to His wisdom, yet often it sits unwrapped and unused. We're just like a kid at Christmas getting a brand-new bike, all wrapped up in a massive box, but we don't really want to open it, being satisfied with a new pair of socks and a new video game instead.

To pray is to interact with the Eternal One—the only person who transcends time and space and who created all things yet, in His innate worthiness, puts all things to shame. Prayer is an invitation into mystery. Do we even know what we're doing when we speak in our rooms alone or whisper in the dark at night or talk softly to a sunset? We're unwrapping a gift more precious than anything the world can offer.

TWO PARTS OF PRAYER

If prayer is interaction and conversation with God, we ought to consider what conversation is. Conversation consists of two parts: listening and speaking. In praying, many people might lean one way or another, but both of these parts are of equal value.

Most of us struggle with only speaking to God—and then coming to Him only to express our own needs. We're like the college student I could have been, only calling Mom or Dad when the bank account was about to be overdrawn. We frame our relationship with God around *our* desires, not His. Do we *feel* like praying? If not, we don't.

We never take into consideration that He might also be speaking to us. In so doing, we abandon our relationship with God and accept an agreement with Him. The more we lean toward a speaking-heavy prayer life, the more we neglect and forget the presence of God and, before long, we realize He no longer feels near.

But for some there's a temptation to listen too much and never speak. You may be thinking, *Who listens to God too much?* Well, as we'll see, listening to God involves reading the Bible—His words. When we read His words, He speaks to us and we receive from Him. And so, there is a possibility we could love Bible study but ignore prayer altogether. There are Christians who are highly interested in theology but never actually speak to the One they're trying to describe. We're like the fan who knows all of the stats about his team's favorite player and, when seeing that athlete at a Starbucks, he makes a fool of himself as he fumbles over words, speaking to someone he does not know, but just knows *about*. When we finally get to a place where we speak to God directly, we have this depressing realization that we really do not know Him well. As this feeling sets in, we realize He no longer feels near. Balance is required.

THE LISTENING PART

If you were to meet with me for discipleship on a regular basis, I would ask you this question every time we met:

"What is God speaking to you?"

I ask this question because I am under the assumption the Bible is under: God is constantly speaking to us.

When we start talking about God talking to us, we may get a little weirded out. God speaking to humans? That seems a bit overly spiritual and eerie. But what if God's voice is found less in a hyper-existential way and more in a practical, sure fashion?

The sad thing is, most Christians disregard the voice of God in their everyday lives. It is remarkable how rarely I hear people talk about what God is teaching them or telling them. When we feel distant from God, it is because we have lost the mindset of hearing God. If the God of the universe *is in fact* speaking to us, wouldn't this transform the human experience altogether?

The Bible describes people hearing from God in two primary ways: His Word (referred to as "law" or "Scripture" or "precepts/rules") and directly from Him—whether through the Holy Spirit, out of the mouth of the Son, or from a thunderous boom of heaven. People throughout Scripture are always hearing from God in multiple ways—what makes us think we would be any different? Certainly we excuse ourselves from the saints of the Old Testament and the apostles, but why? God is our Father—or, to borrow another metaphor, a shepherd—are we not in the perfect position to hear His voice?

We are. Your Bible and your practice of asking the Holy Spirit to speak to you are the single most important spiritual resources you have as a Christian today. Our Bibles go unread and our minds drift into the garbage of modern life as the menial cares of our own little world take over. All the while, God is speaking. Are we listening?

The first way we hear from God in prayer is from His Spirit. From my personal experience, this is rarely (but can be) manifested in an audible voice. Instead, more often God puts impressions on our hearts; He speaks in the silence to us, in a kind of whisper. Many of you have heard this voice during important moments of your life. God actively speaks to His people today, and we must be listening (John 10:27). We need to learn to trust this voice and wait for it, but also to test what we hear with Scripture.

Secondly, we hear from God through His Word. The Bible is more often viewed as a book we need to study so we can know facts. We're told to read our Bibles, to know our Bibles, and to study our Bibles. We are not told to listen to our Bibles. The Bible is not meant to be dissected; it is meant to be heard.

"Let the word of Christ dwell in you richly," says Paul in Colossians 3:16. The psalmist—seemingly obsessed with God's "law" and "word"—says, "I have stored up your word in my heart" (Psalm 119:11). The Bible is meant not only for us to be in, but for it to be in us. There is a "storing up," a "dwelling" to happen—the Word must take residence in our deepest places of being. It is where we learn what God sounds like and discover who He is. Without that, we're without an anchor in a deep and drifting sea.

When I was a little boy, my brother and I were given a "secret word" from my father. This secret word was supposed to protect us from any stranger who did not belong in our company. We grew up in the city and were constantly riding our bikes all over, and I think my dad was trying to form as many layers of protection as possible.

"If anyone approaches you," he said, "and they don't know the secret word, you should not go with them."

Of course the idea was that no one would know the secret word and therefore no one would ever take us, no matter where we were. The purpose of the word was for us to know who we were to be with and who we weren't to be with. This word was known only by my father and mother in order to connect us under shared language. There was nothing special about it *in and of itself*; its only power came from the person who invented it. The secret word was constantly directing me back to the presence of my family, not strangers.

God's Word does this same thing. There is nothing magical about it, nothing superstitious in its nature, but it connects us with God and separates us from temptation, evil, and other anxieties of the world. We are protected from evil and pointed toward our heavenly Father. As I've heard it said before, the Bible is not the point of faith, but it points to the Point of faith.

> God's Word connects us with God and separates us from temptation and anxieties of the world.

I stress the importance of the Bible in this chapter on prayer because I believe we are in desperate need of a

101

healthy love of Scripture. Most of the leaders you may hear stressing the importance of the Bible are actually stressing the importance of *doctrine,* or some set of teaching assembled from traditions. The importance of the Bible goes hand in hand with the importance of prayer, for in the Bible we are hearing the very words of God. Here is where we listen to Him, get to know Him, and better align our hearts to His will and plan for humanity. The Bible is our first place to go when trying to hear from God. Without a good, faithful reading of God's Word, we will never know what His voice sounds like.

This is how the two forms of listening—to His Word (the Bible) and His voice—work together. Scripture opens us to the Holy Spirit, *teaching us to know what God sounds like so we can hear Him more directly.* God's Spirit is a person who speaks, guides, leads, counsels, and provides power to those who believe on the name of Jesus. As we trust Jesus, walk in discipleship, and seek the Father, the Holy Spirit *dwells in us.* It is in this special relationship that God's Word comes alive. The Spirit speaks to us and will always match up with Scripture.

When we are seeking God in prayer—whether listening or speaking to Him—it is important to remember that the words spoken by God are eternal, because God exists as the "Eternal One." This means we will never "hear" something from God in prayer that goes against His written Word, the Bible. As we seek Him in prayer, it is essential for us to have a dynamic, faithful relationship to Scripture so we do not fall into the roaring waves of selfishness and foolishness.

It is sad how we act as if God's voice is not real or available to little old us. We put ourselves in a different category as the people of Scripture and of our tradition, claiming God doesn't speak as He used to in the good old days. And yet Scripture itself tells us, "Elijah was a man with a nature like ours, but he prayed" (James 5:17). Yes, Elijah was just a man, *but he prayed*. He listened to God, he spoke to God, he asked God for things. I wonder if we understood our kinship and likeness to Elijah, could we do the same things he did? The same things the apostles did? I don't see why not.

THE SPEAKING PART

When we listen to God, we do what any normal person does when in a conversational relationship of any sort: we talk back. So prayer is often an uncomfortable and awkward experience for a person who is fourteen or older as they start to believe. I often hear people say in regards to prayer: "I don't think I'm doing it right," as if they are learning to fly a kite.

It's odd to notice how children do not need much guidance when it comes to prayer. Ask a child to pray, and she will simply ask for whatever she needs and say whatever she wants. Children are entirely assuming of God that He loves them and wants to provide for them. Children are the most comfortable in the presence of God and seem to also be quite comfortable in who they are before Him. It is only as we grow older that we feel more awkward before the King. This drives us to ask sheepishly, stumble over the "right" words to say before God, and even lie to God (and ourselves).

And while I love the heart of the child, and while Jesus Himself would instruct us to be as presumptuous as the little ones, His disciples asked what we ask: "Lord, teach us to pray" (Luke 11:1). There is, in fact, an instruction in speaking to God. There is a way we must learn, a school we must attend, and we are in need of it today in our churches and homes.

WAYS OF SPEAKING:
SPEAKING SCRIPTURALLY, OR THE FRUSTRATING
REALITY OF NOT KNOWING WHAT TO SAY

We talk quite a bit about prayer. There is no Christian in America or elsewhere who would say prayer is unimportant. A common phrase is simply, "I'll pray for you," but it is rarely followed up by a prayer right there. Then, when we get to it, we're not sure what to pray for or how to phrase each request. We sit at a desk in an office or lay in our bed or stare at a bowl of cereal while considering the next thing we should say to the Creator of land, sea, and sky. When we do muster up the words, they often don't seem right and we just make something up that sounds good and honest. In our pondering and meandering, our minds wander and our prayer life suffers. We, again, drift from God.

A while ago, my wife pulled out this little book by Dietrich Bonhoeffer called, *Psalms: The Prayer Book of the Bible*. In it, she showed me this quote, which has directed our prayer lives ever since: "The richness of God's Word ought to determine our prayer, not the poverty of the heart."[2]

When my wife read that to me, I realized how many of my prayers come out of a tired heart and restless mind. Not only do I not know what to pray, I pray whatever I feel like and end my prayers when I feel like ending them. Most often, this means my time in prayer is short and lacks any faith.

Bonhoeffer is calling us to do the difficult work of allowing Scripture to pray for us, to look at the Bible and, as Eugene Peterson says, learn to speak God's language so we can "answer God."[3] Peterson and Bonhoeffer direct our prayer lives not to more endless empty speech, but back to the Bible, specifically the Psalms.

Psalms is the only book in the Bible that talks back to God. It is both God's Word to man and man's words to God. Every other book may include a prayer to God, but Psalms is the only book where the various writers address God through the whole thing. Each chapter is filled with verses directed toward God. It is in the Psalms where we learn to answer God as He has spoken to us in His Word and His Holy Spirit.

This is also why, when the disciples asked Jesus to teach them to pray, He didn't tell them, "Try starting with fifteen minutes a day and just say whatever is on your heart to God." That tends to be how we teach people to pray. No, Jesus gave His disciples a script, a way of speaking to God that we call "The Lord's Prayer" today (Matt. 6:9–13; Luke 11:1–4).

Prayer is something that is learned by first repeating the prayers of the people of God in Scripture. It is in the pages of our Bibles where we rehearse particular prayers and learn the type of language God speaks. The way toward a rich prayer life involves picking up your Bible and actually reading God's Word back to Him. When you don't know what to pray, pick a Psalm, and use it as a guide to pray, even when you don't feel like it. Praying the Psalms can entice your heart's affections toward God and help you remember the things you need to ask of God. As Bonhoeffer wrote elsewhere, when we are "grounded in the Scripture, we learn to speak in the language that God has spoken to us. We learn to speak to God as the child speaks to his mother."[4]

SPEAKING HONESTLY, OR THE ART OF IMPROVISATION IN PRAYER

When we pray the Psalms and the Lord's Prayer or any of the other prayers found in Scripture, we are praying richly. Our prayers are now ones the people of God have been praying for centuries—we can have great confidence in their power. But some people might be asking, "Isn't this a bit dishonest? I mean, these aren't *our* words after all. This seems a bit forced."

While I see where you're coming from, isn't it more forced to try to come up with new language that would be effective? Furthermore, aren't there times where our honesty is actually just selfishness masked as "being vulnerable" or "real"? A lot of our talk about our shortcomings and our expressions to God are very self-focused. Prayer becomes shallow when we use a lot of words like "I" or "me" or "my." In the Lord's Prayer, God is addressed four times before the prayer addresses the needs. Prayer is about getting on God's program, not getting God on our program.

I think our honesty should come out after our praying of Scripture. In his excellent book *Prayer: Experiencing Awe and Intimacy with God*, Keller says Scripture (the Psalms and the Lord's Prayer, in particular) can be viewed as the bar chords to which we improvise from—he calls this "spiritual 'riffing.'"[5] Musicians understand that certain songs may have a bass line or a simple chord structure which the rest of the improvising builds off of. This is how Scripture can function in our prayers. The Word of God is our foundation and rhythm from which our prayers are built.

Dallas Willard once told an interviewer that he would take the Lord's Prayer and Psalm 23 line by line as a guide to his prayer life.[6] In other words, when we say, "Our Father in heaven," we can pause there and say something like, "I'm so grateful to be Your child and I ask that you show me more what Your fatherly love looks like." Then, you can pray, "hallowed be thy name, thy kingdom come, thy will be done, on earth as it is in heaven." As you pray this, you can now pray about anything that comes to your mind regarding God's breaking in to this world through His kingdom. This should cause us to think about our schools, families, workplaces, and communities—wherever we desire to see God's reign and rule anew. The Bible then becomes the foundation the rest of our prayer life is built upon. Instead of creating whole prayers and sprinkling some Scripture language on top, we make Scripture our base ingredient.

SPEAKING BOLDLY, OR HOW
TO BE A PRESUMPTUOUS CHILD

As we familiarize ourselves with God's language in Scripture and come before Him with great honesty, there's also this element of boldness, or as I often put it: presumption.

Children are incredibly presumptuous and bold. You can see this every time they do not get what they want the way they want it. To see this in action, spend some time at a public swimming pool. Once in the water, the child desires to swim for the rest of eternity. Children see no reason why they should *stop* swimming—that would be insane! So when Mom comes by and gives the famous "five-minute warning," the child raises objections immediately. Five minutes later, when mom says it's time to go, the child never hesitates to ask for more time—there is always an ask and usually a little fight. In similar fashion, if a child wants a cookie while his mother is getting her afternoon iced coffee, the child will not hesitate to request it and, upon requesting, be certain that he will receive it. If he does not, there may be a little fight.

Children have no problem asking their parents for things because they assume they will get it. Maybe that's because the child knows she has a certain level of access to the parent no one else has. Jesus draws on this when teaching on prayer, saying, "For everyone who asks receives, and the one who seeks finds, and to the one who knocks it will be opened. What father among you, if his son asks for a fish, will instead of a fish give him a serpent. . . . If you then, who are evil, know how to give good gifts to your children, how much more will the heavenly Father give the Holy Spirit to those who ask him!" (Luke 11:10–13).

Unfortunately, as we grow older, we become less expectant or presumptuous of God and more cynical. Other adults in our life fail us, our friends don't come through, and we make a rule about life and set it in stone: people do not fulfill their promises.

This rule transfers to our relationship with God and we stop asking Him for things. It astonishes me how many people I meet who do not ask God for the things they need. "But if God so clothes the grass," Jesus says, "will he not much more clothe you, O you of little faith" (Matt. 6:30)?

When my wife and I were trying to move closer to our church, we began looking for a house in the area. We had been living in a small apartment in the city and were moving south of the city to the small town our church served. I was stressing out about all of the details—how much it would cost, where it would be in relation to the church and a bus line, how big it would be, etc.—when all of a sudden I realized: why don't I put this one on God? I hadn't asked Him for a house.

Thinking this way, I told my wife and we began to pray very simple prayers: "God, if You want us in the community of our church family, please give us a house." This prayer is based in the line from the Lord's Prayer: "Give us this day our daily bread." Jesus teaches us to ask God to provide for us the things we need, including where we will live and what we will eat and drink and wear (Matt. 6:25, 31).

The first two houses we were interested in "fell through." One of them that we had barely lost out on seemed absolutely perfect. The other one was too small and in a weird location and the landlord didn't seem trustworthy. A tempting and cruel thought entered my brain: *is this how it goes when I ask You for something, God?*

For a couple of weeks we felt that our prayers were going unheard. And then a house popped up: cheaper, better, and bigger than anything before. God had provided. This would become the home where we would have many ministry memories: students enjoying a huge backyard, young guys coming to grips with themselves and their faith in my living room, groups of people praying and reading Scripture together, and my wife and I welcoming countless people in to stay the night, and sometimes stay for a long time in our spare room.

Then a house popped up: cheaper, better, and bigger than anything before. God had provided.

The best part about God answering this prayer, though, is that there is never a day where I believe this house to be *my* house. In fact, when I am walking back from the coffee shop near us, I get this great view of the whole place. I am struck with how we can live there—it really seems too good to be true. It seems like a house we could never have on our own. That's because it is. God gave us this house for a short time and it is so clear in my mind that it is not mine. Why? Because He gave it to me. It is God's house, for His purposes and honor.

When we pray with boldness, asking God in faith and presuming He will grant us things, it makes it all the sweeter when He does. And just like when a father gives a gift to a son, my relationship with God increases and I sense His presence in my life more. God's presence enters into my life when I not only ask Him for things, but remember how much He has given my family. It takes discipline and a certain kind of imagination to think through all God has done for us. But if we really want more of God's presence in our lives, this kind of mental practice becomes necessary.

What do you need? Ask God. Ask Him for everything you need. The answer you receive may in fact be "no," and the answer may come later, but the answer will come. He hears you; He will provide for you. The question just remains: do you believe Him? As you see answered prayer in your life, the distance between you and God will close. I am sure of it.

PRACTICING PRAYER DAILY

After that first year in college I wrote about earlier, away from my parents and growing in adulthood, I continued to realize that simple lesson about relationships: no communication means no relationship. I have gone through good times with my parents and not-so-good times since then, and all of those can be attributed to how we were communicating with each other during those particular seasons.

Sometimes, when I sit with someone who feels God is far away, I will ask them: how often are you talking to God? When was the last time you interacted with Him over His Word and pressed toward His Spirit?

Most every Christian will offer up a prayer or two a day, something simple and benign. But I wonder how many of us speak with Him for a long time or every single day. Beyond that, I wonder how many of us are speaking His language, praying the prayers He Himself taught us to pray? Unfortunately, I see an increased number of people treating God like the college kid calling Mom and Dad only when the bank account empties. Would any of us be so bold as to call *that* a healthy relationship? God is our Father, He cares for us, and our role as sons and daughters is to speak with Him, listen to Him, ask Him things, and develop and nurture what our heart really longs for: relationship.

This kind of daily practice of prayer stirs up my love for God, but it also changes how I view myself. When I stand before a holy, beautiful, benevolent God multiple times every day, my own worthlessness begins to appear. I am humbled, for sure, and I am also aware of how short I fall from Him. This is why the art of prayer always leads to the art of confession. The two are seemingly inseparable, and it's the subject of our next chapter.

Chapter 7

CONFESSING/REPENTING

**Beneath all great accomplishments of our
time there is a deep current of despair.**[1]
HENRI NOUWEN

God used to relate to His people in a different way than He
does with us today. Even if the various, substantial cultural
and historical barriers were removed between you and an
ancient Israelite wandering in the desert after the Law was
given, you would have a difficult time understanding each
other when talking about God.

We take for granted that we are living in a remarkable
time in redemptive history. As I said before, living on this
side of the cross gives us the Holy Spirit and access to this
inaccessible God—the temple is destroyed, the curtain is
torn in two, and we now can enjoy the presence of God
through our Mediator, Jesus Christ.

It wasn't always this way.

Actually, it wasn't even close. Today, we relate with God
and speak to others about God on a very *individual* level—
it's about our own personal experience. When we think about

faith in God, we think about *our* faith in God and not our family or our nation. But those living in ancient Israel related to God as a community. They were the people of God and the only way they related to God was as a nation, a corporate community of people who had a relationship with Him simply because He chose all of them together (Deut. 7:6–8).

Additionally, Israel related to God through their sacrifices, whereas we relate to God through the sacrifice of His Son and our spiritual sacrifices (Rom. 12:1–2; Heb. 13:15–16). When Israel distanced themselves from God through sin, they confessed, offered sacrifices, and recommitted to the Law of Moses. When we distance ourselves from God through sin, we confess our sin and claim the work of Jesus on the cross as the final sacrifice and the perfect One who obeyed the Law on our behalf.

Clearly, because of Jesus Christ, God has changed the way in which He relates with His people (Heb. 1:1–4). God has further revealed Himself to us by way of His Son, and we now experience a relationship with Him solely by the work of Christ. While the people of Israel related to God through *awaiting* the Messiah who would come, we have the benefit of *looking back* on the Messiah who has come (Matt. 13:17; Gal. 3:1–14). And yet, there are also some similarities in how God desires to relate to human beings—maybe more than you would think.

A CONNECTION POINT BETWEEN ISRAEL AND US

One of those similarities is clear when reading through Leviticus. I know Leviticus is not the most popular book, but when you are a pastor in seminary you find yourself reading every part of the Bible. (For that matter, I would suggest a reading of Leviticus anyway in a good study Bible.)

Throughout Leviticus, God is outlining His Law, which was given to the people of Israel because they did not know how to obey God on their own, and they were in great need of guidance and protection from their own selfishness. The Law was a gift because it helped the people know God was near to them and that they were His distinct people.

The book includes provisions and protections for sin and wrongdoing. With every sin, there is an ability to make sacrifice or an offering to right the relationship with God and one another. There are rules that govern religious, societal, and cultural practice—all available to them by God's great grace. After all, He didn't have to give them the Law as a guide; He could have let them wander off and be alienated from Him. Instead, He reached out with a way back—His laws.

At twenty-seven chapters, the book is long and, for the most part, boring and at times almost incomprehensible. And yet, near the end of the book, Leviticus 26, Moses summarizes all of the Law and the practice God desires for His people. Before the people of Israel, the Almighty God sets up His blessings for them if they choose to obey (vv. 1–13) and then tells them the curses they will experience if the people disobey Him (vv. 14–39).

The final verses in God's Law concern His people's disobedience and are blunt: "You shall perish among the nations, and the land of your enemies shall eat you up. And those of you who are left shall rot away in your enemies' lands because of their iniquity, and also because of the iniquities of their fathers they shall rot away like them" (26:38–39).

While it appears to be harsh, the teaching of the Old Testament is simple: when we do not trust God and follow His ways, destruction comes to us, whether by God, ourselves, or mankind. Here in Leviticus (and also Deuteronomy), God warns that His people will not last long if they disobey; other nations will conquer them and punish them. Unfortunately, this would all prove to be quite prophetic for Israel.

Nevertheless, the book does not end here. At this point, if you've been reading Leviticus as a normal book from start to finish, you would think God would now say, "OK, but if you mess this up, here are sacrifices, festivals, and offerings you can give in order to get you back." That's the way it works and it seems appropriate to place here, too. The people would offer sacrifices in order to cover their sins, restoring their relationship with Yahweh, their God. Isn't this yet another opportunity to cover up and heal their sin?

It is, but God says something different and surprising: "But if they confess their iniquity and the iniquity of their fathers in their treachery that they committed against me, and also in walking contrary to me . . . if then their uncircumcised heart is humbled and they make amends for their iniquity, then I will remember my covenant with Jacob" (vv. 40–42).

Did you catch this? A humble heart and a confession is

all God is looking for from a wandering, dissatisfied, broken people. God desires an acknowledgment of wrongdoing and selfishness and a busted up heart (Psalm 51:17).

> A humble heart and a confession is all God is looking for from a wandering, broken people.

It reminds me of the end to another big Old Testament book, Isaiah. In 66:2, God, through the prophet Isaiah, has this simple, beautiful desire for restoration: "But this is the one to whom I will look: he who is humble and contrite in spirit and trembles at my word."

God is looking for a heart that is broken and recognizes its crooked ways in light of God's perfection. I think one of the reasons I have drifted from God in the past is simply because I have stopped confessing this aspect of myself to Him regularly. Yet another book ends with a call to confession—it's the book of James: "Therefore, confess your sins to one another and pray for one another, that you may be healed" (James 5:16).

If confession is so central to God's relationship with His creation, why do we neglect it so often?

CONFESSING TO OTHERS AND FINDING GOD

Just as the Bible calls us to "abide" in Christ through loving obedience and prayerful living, it also calls us to humble confession in the midst of it all. This is because God knows we will not perfectly keep His ways. He knows that we will be unsteady in our prayers and lack long-term ability to obey Him perfectly. How come we so often try to challenge this fact?

One of my heroes is the twentieth-century German theologian and pastor Dietrich Bonhoeffer, who stood against Hitler's regime during World War II. In his remarkable book on community called *Life Together*, he wrote, "He who is alone with his sin is utterly alone." In this context, Bonhoeffer is showing how confession brings us close to our brothers and sisters, but I also see this as true between us and God. Later Bonhoeffer added, "When I go to my brother to confess, I am going to God."[2]

I find it easy to confess to God privately—and I think it's necessary to do so. But I also think many of us *only* privately confess to God in our heads instead of confessing to our community. Because we now host the Holy Spirit in our bodies as believers, when we come together we are actually Christ's body, the church. Bonhoeffer is getting at the important reality: our confession to others *is also a confession to Christ.*

Our confessions should be regular within the body of Christ and to the people we have hurt. By confessing to those in our church family, we can experience the grace of Jesus as they look us in the eye without judgment. When I confess my own sin to brothers and sisters, I open myself to receive a special kind of grace.

Furthermore, our confessions need to involve those we have directly hurt—no matter if they are Christian or not. Just as confessing to the church family opens me to grace, confessing to the individuals I have hurt opens me to reconciliation. When we practice this kind of open confession, we can experience God in magnificent ways. If we refuse to speak to one another with candor and humility, confessing our sins and receiving grace and reconciliation, how will we grow in Christlikeness? Grace and reconciliation are at the heart of the gospel. Is it possible that by refusing to confess we have also refused the offer of Christ's presence? Where there is grace and truth, there He is.

Could it be that you and I are missing out on God's presence not *because* we sin, but because we do not *acknowledge* our sin before God and those we offend? Look back at that verse in James 5. We're told when we confess, we will "be healed." Healing and restoration and joy of the presence of God does not come through flawless obedience (that is impossible), but through confession, dependence, and humility, because these actions are essential parts of obeying Him.

CONFESSION TODAY

My generation, often referred to as "millennials," holds authenticity and vulnerability as its highest values. We love "being true to yourself" and "just being you." When someone speaks truthfully and honestly, we praise them. This is a great thing. I can remember one of my older leaders at a middle school camp one year being shocked at the number of kids sharing dark, hidden hurts through the week. She was overwhelmed. As she sat sharing this, confused and broken for the kids, another leader said, "Yeah, the vulnerability is incredible, but isn't it amazing that kids are finally seeing the church as the place to confess?" I realized we're living in an important cultural moment as students were beginning to be honest within the community of Christ.

And yet, *confession* is different than vulnerability and honesty. Confession is admitting your wrongdoing, being crushed by the weight of the sin in your own experience, and offering that to God and others. While my generation is obsessed with vulnerability, we need help with confession. Confession is taking our vulnerable experience and identifying the "wrongness" (or, the "sin") within it. We don't just share *that* we have sinned, we reveal our inability to make ourselves right through morality and behavior modification. "Sin" is not just something we do, it is a disease within us from which we must be healed.

We might "open up" about sleeping with someone who is not our wife, but not feel the devastation inside that and how we need God's help to make us right. We might say "I did something I regret," but we must then take it to the next place where we understand the offense our actions are to God and the world and ourselves. Confession involves a type of grief. And "godly grief produces a repentance that leads to salvation," Paul says in 2 Corinthians 7:10. This grief and recognition of our own sin leads to a deliverance, a freeing of ourselves that leads to restored fellowship with God (1 John 1:9).

My generation is missing out on experiencing the full, loving presence of God because we are too proud to truly confess our sins to God. We want to be vulnerable, but not holy and Christlike. I have had the joy of seeing how close God comes when people confess; it is a remarkable experience that cannot be replaced. Some of the greatest moments in my marriage have come as my wife and I are praying and offering confessions to God.

While we pride ourselves on Bible study and devotions, sending Instagrams of our hikes and sharing how close to God we feel in a sunset, I am afraid we're missing an over-flow of His presence by refusing to confess. Don't get me wrong, I feel immensely close to God in nature and Bible study, but it pales in comparison to confession. This is because in confession we do not get less of God's love, but more. The unbe-lievable grace of God means we do not get *less* love from God as we tell Him our weaknesses, *we get all the more.*

> We miss the merciful, cleansing, and powerful presence of God when we conceal our sins.

We are missing the merciful, cleansing, and powerful presence of God when we conceal our sins and treat them as not that big of a deal. When we say, "God will forgive me later," and we willingly commit sin, we settle for a small God who is simply there to wish away the bad and make us feel good. God does not ask us to reveal our sins so that He might shame us and point it out; He asks us to reveal our sins so He might prove His great love for us. Like a nasty wound under a bandage, no good doctor pulls the bandage off to look at it and laugh. No, the bandage is removed so the medicine can be applied. Likewise, God asks us to uncover our sin so we can witness the power of His love poured over all our unworthiness. If we never confess sin, we will never fully know God loves us, because we will only understand the version of love received from our church family.

Confession has power to restore our relationship and make us depend on Christ. As the apostle John writes, "If we confess our sins, he is faithful and just to forgive us our sins and cleanse us from all unrighteousness" (1 John 1:9). Paul recounts Jesus visiting him in a time of pain in this way: "But he said to me, 'My grace is sufficient for you, for my power is made perfect in weakness.' Therefore I will boast all the more gladly of my weaknesses, so that the power of Christ may rest upon me" (2 Cor. 12:9). And in the Old Testament book of Proverbs, there is a wise saying similar to John's: "People who conceal their sins will not prosper, but if they confess and turn from them, they will receive mercy" (Prov. 28:13 NLT). When we are weak in confession before God and others in our church family, we receive more of God's power. If you've ever experienced this before, you know it is quite a wonderful feeling.

TOWARD A COMMUNITY OF CONFESSION

There is no way for us to move ahead in confession without great boldness. The writer of Hebrews encourages us to go boldly to God because of what Jesus has done (Heb. 4:16). We must have great confidence as we approach God, not desiring to get clean before we come, but come so that we may be cleaned. We just have to do it—we must begin confessing.

Additionally, this will require pastors like me to lead in confession and receiving confession. I remember God speaking this to me so clearly when a student of mine came out of the closet and confessed he was gay. In his confession at a night of prayer, I sensed God's Holy Spirit speaking to me as if to say, "Chris, this is a moment to show this kid grace and mercy. He has been bold, now you must be bold enough to show him *My mercy*. You are My representative!" I hugged this young kid and told him I loved him and began to pray that God would pour out His love in that moment, that God would prove His grace to be powerful and real. Our tears were a testimony to God not shaming this student or me in that moment, but revealing His love in spite of our sin.

I think some of us are not getting the vast picture of God's love—seen in such passages as Ephesians 3:18–19 and Romans 8:31–38—because we have not seen how huge God's love is *in the midst of sin*. We all believe God will love us *after* we are sinners, but we forget God has loved us *while* we are sinners (Eph. 2:1–10, Rom. 5:8). Do you know this love? Or do you continue to feel as if God is not near? God is near—He awaits your honest confessions, your humility, and your broken heart. As you confess regularly with those filled with God's Spirit, your soul will wake up to the fact that He's been there all along. You just may need some reminding.

Chapter 8

PREACHING/RECEIVING

Why are you cast down, O my soul?
PSALM 43:5

It's difficult to find any lessons about faith and life when you're about to get your wisdom teeth removed, but I must thank New York City pastor Tim Keller for my ability to see something of value as I went under right before a stranger pried four teeth out of the back of my mouth. On the fourth floor of a corporate tower in the heart of northeast Portland, near the intersection of all the city's light rail transportation, my doom awaited.

The fears associated with the wisdom teeth removal surgery are probably as common and benign as the surgery itself. Everyone tells you horror stories, but it's difficult to meet a person whose entire life has changed because of some complication of the procedure. Nevertheless, anxiety abounds.

I was seventeen and had recently discovered Pastor Keller and his sermon archive for online purchase. About a month before the surgery I listened as he talked about surgery on his neck to remove a cancerous mass. He was telling the story to illustrate the relationship between knowledge and faith—two things people often think are disconnected.

He shared about how the only thing that kept his fears at bay was not thinking *less* about the surgery and the surgeon, but more. He needed to talk to himself, proclaiming truth about the surgeon: *these are professionals; they do this every day, multiple times every day, and are highly successful.* The more thinking about the surgery, the less afraid Keller became. *This surgeon has been practicing for years and is one of the most qualified people in his field.*

I took the same approach as I sat in the chair awaiting the surgeon to come in and do his thing: *this is routine, he will do many of these same surgeries today, millions of people have gone through this, and he has helped them get through it. He's a pro. He knows what he is doing. Relax.*

Faith and knowledge go hand in hand: when God *feels* distant it does not necessarily *mean* He is distant. As we've been discovering, the more we pay attention to His constant nearness through obedience, the more we will have the opportunity to sense it, feel it, and know Him more deeply. More often than not, our faith is weak because we have forgotten God and lost our mind toward Him. We lack trust in Him, we're afraid about the future, and unsure if He will come through.

The human tendency at this point is to *stop* thinking. To trust experience and "blind faith." We try to read our Bible, we struggle through prayers, and our anxiety only grows as all of our attempts fall flat. But these are the moments to think harder than ever and press further in. Just like before going into surgery, thinking *more* helped the peace come, and I think the same thing needs to happen in our relationship with God.

PREACHING TO YOURSELF

After successful oral surgery and a lesson about faith, I came across a phrase used by John Piper in his book *When I Don't Desire God* (a book I would, for the most part, recommend to many of you reading this). In the book, Piper teaches the reader to "preach to yourself,"[1] which is precisely what Keller and I did before entering surgery.

It sounds like a strange practice, but preaching to yourself becomes essential in our life of faith, especially after we have gone through confession, which we looked at in the last chapter.

When we confess our sin, it can be easy to think God's love and mercy cannot handle it. Or, on the flip side, we can think that the confession is all we need, instead of our confession leading us to repentance and a changed life. But when we preach the great gospel to ourselves, we are reminded, nothing can "separate us from the love of God in Christ Jesus our Lord" (Romans 8:39).

Preaching to yourself may take many forms, but in the end these mini sermons are simply self-dictated and self-addressed phrases of truth. My favorite biblical example of someone preaching to themselves is Psalm 43:5, where the writer says, "Why are you cast down, O my soul . . . ? Hope in God." Notice the psalmist is not talking to God or to some community; he's talking to himself—preaching to himself. He's asking himself questions and telling himself (specifically, telling his soul) to put his hope in the God of Israel, the only one who can save and who has always saved those who walk in His ways and remain faithful.

Think about how many times you see the word "remember" in the Old Testament. This is because the Old Testament writers (particularly the prophets) are asking the people of God to *think* and be reminded of the good God has always done, especially in saving His people from Egypt. "You shall remember that you were a slave in the land of Egypt, and the Lord God brought you out from there with a mighty hand and an outstretched arm" (Deut. 5:15). A huge part of the law and the Sabbath was for the people of Israel to be reminded and preach to themselves the reliability of their God, that He is the faithful one.

Most of the Jewish practices of feasts, festivals, and laws regarding sacrifice, were all simple ways for the people to "remember" things God had done for them. Their rituals, like the Passover meal, had one purpose: to remember that YHWH (transliterated Yahweh, or "the LORD") was the one who faithfully brought them out of slavery (Deut. 16:1–8). Much of Jewish religious practice centered around this word: *remember* (v. 3). God asks people to set up monuments, memorials, and altars so they may never forget who God is and what He has done. He seems to know what we do not: that we will forget.

Today, we must make this a practice, constantly reminding ourselves of the gospel—the good news that Jesus has come and finished the work of bringing the presence of

God into our individual lives through the Holy Spirit. As Jesus was teaching His disciples about the Eucharist (or "Communion") meal, He told them, "Do this in remembrance of me" (Luke 22:19). We are His people, we are His children, and we are not just awaiting the day of His return, but we are remembering the day of His first coming, because through the cross "His divine power has granted to us all things that pertain to life and godliness" (2 Pet. 1:3). What amazing promises. We must remember them and preach their truths to our own souls.

WHAT WE *WILL* FORGET

Throughout every year of working with students, we try to provide them with experiences where they can learn from God and encounter Him in new ways. Through camps, missions trips, and retreats, it is highly likely you'll see multiple social media posts every year talking about a week a student "will never forget." When we experience God in a new way, it is a profound and eternal moment, and it's easy to believe we will never forget how we felt and what we learned.

Whenever I hear people say this, I quickly correct them: "You will forget," I say. This normally takes the person aback for a second and that's when I remind them about their heart: it is deceitful and tricky. Six months or six weeks or six days after that moment, we will find ourselves discouraged for one reason or another, and we will ask the question the Serpent asked in the garden of Eden: "Did God really . . . ?" His questions and our doubts come at us unexpectedly:

Was that actually God you felt . . . ?

It was probably just an emotional moment.

Would God really call YOU to THAT . . . ?

That was all in my head.

There's no way that was real.

Is that really what happened . . . ?

These are the lines that fill our heads in the darker moments of our spiritual life. Things don't always make sense when we look back—hindsight is not always 20/20.

This is why I am a huge fan of writing things down. I keep two notebooks with me most of the time. The first is a really small notebook where I write little notes to myself about prayer. Sometimes it is just a word or a quick phrase, other times it is longer. I write prayers I am praying and little notes when they are answered or being answered. When I get discouraged, I can look and see what God is actually doing. Most of the time I am surprised to read a simple fact the Bible teaches: God answers more prayers than you think.

The second notebook is larger and is the one I take notes in from sermons and write longer stories in. When someone responds to the gospel or I have a crazy moment where the Spirit lines things up perfectly, I report it in the journal. It is not elegant or well-written, but that's OK, it is recorded and that is all that matters. When I get the time to look back and read during times of discouragement and doubt, I read so many things I realize I have forgotten. I find myself a bit embarrassed to have lost my hope and trust in God and I inevitably end up preaching to myself: "Chris, God is good and faithful, He has done so much . . . keep placing your trust in Him. He will provide and come through!"

"Write what you see," Jesus tells John in Revelation 1:11, and I think we should do the same thing. From the Old Testament to the final book in the New Testament, people are writing down the things of God to remember so that they may receive the preached word that God is faithful.

A BRIEF NOTE ON CHURCH ATTENDANCE

Be careful in talking about church attendance amongst twenty-first-century Christians. Right when you mention it, they will get nervous, thinking you're trailing into being legalistic or a fundamentalist. "Church" has become loosely defined as anything from a traditional mass to a husband and wife reading the Bible in their pajamas on Sunday morning.

If we desire to live close to God, we cannot ignore His family. If you came to my house and complimented me on everything in my house, but suddenly started critiquing my wife, I would ask you to leave and we would not be friends. You can't love Jesus and be critical of His bride.

"Going to church" is not the best description of what we're actually doing. We are joining with brothers and sisters from all walks of life to hear God's word, worship His great name, and practice humility together. We may fancy ourselves a better person than the pastor, but hopefully in attending church regularly the Spirit would work that pride out. We may not love the music, but in time He will teach us what the American church must learn: worship, by its very nature, is not about us at all.

Church attendance grows us, humbles us, and shapes us because we hear God's word, worship, and partake in His supper. Church services become effective and helpful when we become more humble and aware of God's grandeur. Missing church isn't just missing a sermon, it is missing an opportunity to rehear the gospel in a variety of formats, whether it be through music, prayer, preaching, communion, or a neighbor.

THE CONTINUAL NEED FOR THE GOSPEL

To a run-down, discouraged, sin-ridden church in Corinth, Paul begins the conclusion of his letter this way: "Now I would remind you, brothers, of the gospel I preached to you" (1 Cor. 15:1). This church knew the gospel, they had responded to the gospel in faith—that's what made them Christians. Their issue was they forgot the gospel and needed to be reminded of its power. Paul takes time to remind them of Jesus' work on the cross and tells them how His death and resurrection changes us and makes us fully human and fully alive.

The book of Hebrews serves as a series of warnings, the first of which we have quoted before: "Therefore *we must pay much closer attention to what we have heard,* lest we drift away from it" (Heb. 2:1, emphasis added). Look at those words of "remind" and "pay . . . attention" in the 1 Corinthians and Hebrews verses.

I don't see a lot of Christians using these words in counseling one another and encouraging one another. I see more believers frustrated and complaining about how their church isn't "going deep" in messages, but what is more deep than applying the gospel to our lives and encouraging one another to hope in God? We want to know more historical background of certain passages, parse Greek or Hebrew words, and study ancient archaeology of lost cities. These things can be helpful to certain passages, but it is all complementary to the Word. None of that will transform us into people of humility and integrity. Only the gospel of Jesus and the Holy Spirit of God can do that. The gospel is the multifaceted, beautiful, simple message of God's generous love being extended to us in Jesus Christ. We need to preach this to ourselves again and again.

Many of us hear someone say, "the gospel," and we immediately say, "Oh, I know that . . . tell me about something I don't know." When this starts to happen, the dangerous practice of assumption begins. When we assume we know every part of the good news, we will turn off when it is preached. The reality is, we need the gospel in every part of our lives and we need to be constantly reapplying it, always following through on our decision to follow Christ and understanding how we might know Him more. Paul says, "I press on toward the goal for the prize of the upward call of God in Christ Jesus" (Phil. 3:14). To the church in Ephesus he says the love of God "surpasses knowledge" (Eph. 3:19). These phrases make me think there is no time when we should just say, "Yeah, I got that" or, "I'll take it from here," when it comes to the deep realities of our faith.

When you are struggling to pay close attention to God, maybe you need to "write what you have seen" like Jesus told the apostle John in Revelation. Maybe you need to preach to yourself the reality of God's great love for all mankind, including you. Pick up a pen, grab a journal, and write *to yourself*. Sit with an open Bible in your room, look out the window, and speak to yourself out loud the truths of Scripture. Like the psalmist, say, "Hey, soul, hope in God! His love is never ending and His generosity extends to all people in sin and shame and brings them to freedom! Can't you get that?!" It might seem new or even weird, but it is an ancient practice the people of God have been participating in for ages. They needed to be reminded; what makes you think you won't?

Chapter 9

FEASTING/FASTING

All things in this world are gifts from God.
ST. IGNATIUS OF LOYOLA[1]

Across Seattle's Fremont Bridge, past the busy neighbor-hood record stores, coffee shops, ethnic restaurants, and small huddles of yuppie moms pushing luxury strollers, there is a sandwich stand. Typically the line to that stand winds around the block. Once the wait is over, customers may be holding the most delicious Cubano they have ever tasted. I struggle to write those words knowing I currently sit 191 miles away from its majesty.

Can we agree food has a spiritual element to it? Whether it's a gourmet sandwich at a park or a relaxing meal at a restaurant, think about how many belly-aching laughs you've had sitting at a huge table with friends. How often have you exchanged important moments and words while sitting over a meal with someone you really cared about?

Our previous chapters have brought us along a journey featuring some pretty typical spiritual subjects, like prayer, confession, and Scripture reading. Why all of a sudden am I writing about sandwiches?

The Bible speaks about food more than you may know. When we think about food and spirituality, we Christians can often think only about *fasting*—abstaining from food in order to connect with God—or its opposite, *gluttony*—overindulging in food until we are sick.

These two extremes of feast and famine are often not thought about when talking about God's presence because it makes us a little uncomfortable. We don't want to eat less, because in America we love to indulge. Sometimes we feel guilty for eating a lot, and other times fasting seems a bit overly spiritual.

But an essential Christian understanding is that our bodies are not entirely separate from our souls—they are more connected than we think (see 1 Cor. 6:18–19). This is why sexual sin or murder is made to be such a big deal—it is a spiritual *and* physical offense. On the flip side, this is why God talks to His people about food *a lot*.

Throughout the Old Testament, God interacted with His people through food. Dietary restrictions, animal sacrifices, and feasts all helped the people of Israel find their place in relationship with God. For many of us who now connect with God through the cross, our ability to see God's presence in relationship to our physical experiences has been lost.

SEEING GOD

Much of my early education happened at Catholic schools, and during middle school and high school, my first experience of academically studying the Bible came alongside Jesuit priests. Unlike the common story you may hear, I actually thoroughly enjoyed the Catholic Church's rich history of intellectual rigor, particularly that of the Jesuits. My time spent in the Catholic educational system is a period I look back on with fondness.

The Jesuit priests I interacted with would say the strangest things. I can remember a priest speaking about his process of ordination and saying, "We're not allowed to touch the Bible until we learn how to think." They all took years of philosophy before biblical studies. I liked hearing them talk.

The Jesuits are a Catholic order started by St. Ignatius of Loyola. The Jesuits draw heavily on Ignatius's theology and philosophy of ministry, which emphasizes social justice and spiritual disciplines, which Ignatius called "exercises."

But one of St. Ignatius's landmark teachings (and therefore the Jesuits's as well) was that of "seeing God in all things."[2] While this can seem pantheistic, when you read Ignatius you see his point is more closely tied to the apostle Paul: "So, whether you eat or drink, or whatever you do, do all to the glory of God" (1 Cor. 10:31). The teaching is not that "God is everything" like the pantheists believe, but rather that in every moment there is an opportunity to meet God, no matter what you're doing.

There is a common understanding that we should do things *for* the glory of God, but Paul tells us to direct action toward a preexisting reality he calls, "the glory of God." Our orientation and direction should be faced *toward* God or *toward* His glory. So whatever we eat or drink or see should have its orientation *toward* God and His glory. Similarly Paul tells the Colossian church, "And whatever you do . . . do everything in the name of the Lord Jesus" (Col. 3:17). Doing something "to the glory of God" or "in the name of Jesus" are ways Paul urged his congregations to imagine the vastness of God in our lives.

The Jesuits taught me to not limit God to churches and Bible studies, but to seek Him in the world He created. I often lack the faith to direct all of my life toward God's glory and Jesus' name. I know how to do that in a church, but what does it look like to find God in all things?

EATING BEFORE THE LORD

And this brings us to eating. Across all cultures, time, and nations, eating a meal together changes the relationship because it brings intimacy. When Moses repeats and summarizes the Law of God to His people in Deuteronomy, there is a reminder about how worship will look. To us, we might think this section of the Law would be about singing, but it's actually about eating.

God tells His people in Deuteronomy 12 that they should not just settle anywhere to worship, but that He will show them a place where they will experience His presence and worship Him (vv. 12:4–5). After He shows them this place, His command is simple: "And there you shall bring your burnt offerings and your sacrifices, your tithes and the contribution that you present . . . And there you shall eat before the Lord your God, and you shall rejoice, you and your households, in all that you undertake, in which the Lord your God has blessed you" (vv. 12:6–7).

The first form of worship involves a meal. This was a key way the Israelites communed. Think about the event of the Passover. The whole story was to be told and retold constantly throughout Jewish generations by partaking in the Passover *Meal* (Ex. 12:1–51, Lev. 23:4–8). God uses food as a way to remind us of His goodness in our lives.

Similarly, we take Communion (a meal) regularly (each week or month) to remember the work of Jesus on the cross. When Jesus had the Last Supper, He reminded His disciples that when they ate they should "do this in remembrance of me" (Luke 22:19). The early church "devoted themselves . . . to the breaking of bread" in order to remember God's goodness to one another constantly (Acts 2:42–47). The early church would call these feasts *agape* feasts (or "love feasts," translated from the Greek). The community of believers would come together, decorating tables and serving good food to the entire assembly.

Each week in the summer our church youth group and I leave our space of worship and teaching and go straight to a meal. Dozens of adult volunteers set up, cook, and clean for over two hundred high school students on Wednesday nights. Why? We believe a deeply spiritual way of showing love to people is through giving them a meal and spending time with them. It's that simple.

> We need to learn to connect with God amid friends around a table.

Remember, feasting and fasting before the Lord is not a new thing, but something the people of God have always understood, and it seems to be something we need to understand again.

One of the reasons our generation might be beginning to "feel" distant from God is because we lack the imagination to remember Him. We are so obsessed with perfecting a "spiritual life" that we have lost our regular life. We wait for God in church, yes, or when we read our Bible or pray, but we also need to learn to connect with God and find His presence amid friends around a table, at lunch with family, or even in a late night food run with roommates. (Yes, it can happen that way too.)

We lack the ability to "see God in all things," as St. Ignatius wrote. We need the faith to understand His grace when waiting for the chicken to come out of the oven. God is not restricted to temples and churches (Acts 7:48–50), but exists as the Glorious One in heaven seated on the throne, ready to seek and find His people through His Holy Spirit's presence in regular life. And so whatever we do, we can do *to* that very glory and *in* His name. We must understand this in order to not lose sight of God and drift away.

FEASTING IN HIS PRESENCE

As the table receives its final offering—whether it be whipped garlic mashed potatoes, spicy cilantro and lime rice, or seasoned grilled asparagus—and when each member of the party awaits what will prove to be a gut-filling feast, what goes through your mind? As a host, my proclivity is toward making sure everyone and everything is in its right place. I desire not only for the food to be good, but the experience to be flawless. I find myself anxious for how I might perform amidst the table chatter and worrying about embarrassing myself as I so often do. What I am not always thinking about is how privileged I am. In other words, I am not always grateful.

Next time you find yourself on the precipice of a great meal, practice the discipline of gratitude. Instead of offering empty prayers and reaching for whatever you might believe could be "the right thing to pray," simply stop and thank God for it all. That's it. It's OK to not ask God for anything and instead thank Him for everything. He provides for us our meals and it is perfectly appropriate to skip the whole "bless this food to our bodies" thing (whatever that may mean) and just express your gratitude to God.

Gratitude is at the heart of the discipline of feasting. It pulls God into an area we like to excuse Him from: the dinner table. Often at meals we want to watch television, play on our phones, make crass jokes, or spill the latest gossip to our friends, even as we eat the good food we feel entitled to. It's not as if by doing this we all of a sudden become particularly bad people, we are just missing out on seeing God in all things and allowing His intimate presence near us. When we lack the ability to welcome God into our feasting by being grateful for His provision, He will feel distant. This is not because *He* left, but because we didn't put Him on the guest list. Instead let us remember to feast in His presence.

Our temptation at the table is to be our own providers, enjoying our time with family and friends and leaving God in the church. We are missing some of the most sacred moments with God when we eat alone instead of feasting with

Him. Our practice should imitate the people of Israel: we should eat before the Lord.

WHAT YOU ARE NOT PROMISED

It's a hot night in the middle of July in Tucson, where maybe a hundred students and I have been learning from the poor and underserved immigrant communities for the past four days, with four days to go. I should not be complaining. The hotel lobby chair surrounding me is itself surrounded by cool air from an air conditioning unit the size of a 747. This should make any conversation with any student actually pleasant. One of the students, Michael, approaches me with a tired look.

"Chris," he begins pathetically, "I'm starving."

Michael is not starving. Michael ate lunch *and* dinner that day, and has drunk probably thirty gallons of water. His statement irritates me a little bit. Whenever we go on these trips, we take hundreds of students and the problems are endless: dehydration, social drama, logistic mess-ups, administrative nightmares, and behavior problems only begin the list. But that's all part of the adventure, isn't it?

I was irritated by Michael's comment at first, but the more his words turned over in my mind the more I was convicted: I had never taught these students about feasting and fasting. I had journeyed with them for years and had never given them the opportunity to meet God in a good meal or in a famished state of fasting. Since that moment with Michael, we discuss food as a part of our missions trip training. Most of my students are never hungry, they never

142

feel the pangs of hunger that most of the world includes in their daily life. Because of this, we have an inaccurate view of food and we become gluttonous without ever knowing it. We serve our stomachs and never let them be unsatisfied.

Though most of us are privileged, well-fed Americans, we should be grateful in our feasting, for *we are not promised another meal*. This thought is difficult for me; from my house I can walk to a twenty-four-hour supermarket. It's difficult to believe I am a few meals away from death when I'm constantly full. The difficult work of gratitude is always worth it: to remember that we are not starving and that there will be another meal God provides for us as we trust Him.

I think of Jesus' words now, "do not worry, saying, 'What shall we eat?' or 'What shall we drink?' or 'What shall we wear?' For the pagans run after all these things, and your heavenly Father knows that you need them. But seek first his kingdom and his righteousness, and all these things will be given to you as well" (Matt. 6:31–33 NIV). Because you're not promised to always be full, be grateful to be full and await God's presence in your life to appear as your gratitude.

FASTING: TAKE AWAY AND RECEIVE

Growing up in the Catholic tradition, fasting was a very familiar thing to me. During Lent, the season before Easter, many Catholics fast for long periods of time and give up one or two items they normally rely on, like coffee or sugar.

I remember talking with a priest at my high school

one day during Lent. By this time, I had left the Catholic Church but still enjoyed my lengthy conversations with the Jesuits who inhabited our halls and classrooms. The priest was asking me about what I was giving up for Lent.

"Chocolate," I told him.

"Hm." He stroked his beard. "And what are you engaging in instead of chocolate?"

"What?" I said. I was confused.

He repeated the question: "What are you engaging in instead of chocolate?"

"Nothing. . . . I guess other food?" I said hesitantly.

"Lent is not just about deleting certain foods from your life. It's about deleting *so you can add* more of the holy and sacred to your daily life."

This is the more important question before us as we think about fasting. What are you engaging in? As you take something away, what are you increasing in your life? Many of the students I instruct in fasting do not like the idea of not eating. But often I will ask them, "Do you want more of God? Would you like to add more of God in your life right now?" The answer is always yes and my response is always the same: "Then take away something for a little while."

"Fasting unto our Lord is . . . feasting—feasting on him and on doing his will."[3] There is a kind of feasting that requires fasting and a kind of eating that requires abstaining from any food. We abstain from food so that we might obtain the presence of God.

When I fast, I always have the same realization: eating takes a lot of time in my day. When that time is taken away and replaced with hunger pangs, I find myself in lots of prayer. I also find God to be very faithful in those days when I do not eat. Sometimes I worry about my energy level and then God provides energy. Other times I worry about being short with people due to my lack of food, but God provides the patience. I also get anxious about people thinking weird things about me or it being awkward if someone were to ask me to lunch, but God provides the circumstances.

Let me ask you this: as I watch God provide in all of these ways and my prayer life increases, do you think I end the day feeling near to God? Absolutely. Abstaining from food allows us to obtain Jesus in a new way: to engage Him with gratitude, attentiveness, and humility.

Do you really want to feel close to God—near to Him in a way like never before? I suggest you fast regularly. Fasting is a wonderful example of how I feel about most of Jesus' teachings: you won't get it until you do it.

"AND WHEN YOU FAST"

I can sit hunched over my computer as I am now and think of the many ways to inspire you to fast, but there is nothing like just giving it a shot. I love how Jesus begins His teaching on fasting: "And when you fast . . . " (Matt. 6:16). The thing we overlook about the Sermon on the Mount's teaching on fasting is that Jesus is assuming you are doing it already. It is difficult for me to instruct you in a spiritual discipline you have never practiced.

You need not start with a three-day fast—that would be

unwise. I suggest to people to do what I do most often: a simple twelve- or fourteen-hour fast from sunup to sundown. Wake up early and eat a small breakfast, go through the day with just water, and eat when the sun has gone down. Certainly in my part of the world this is not much of a problem during winter months, but maybe that's where you need to start. Wherever you may be, start somewhere, abstaining from food so that you might obtain God. You won't get it until you do it.

SEEING GOD AGAIN

My wife recently showed me an adorable video of a baby putting her much-needed glasses on for the first time. As her pink, bendable glasses situated in front of her eyes, her entire face changed as the world before her lit up with crisp images and movement. Her world came alive. Something needed to be added, new lenses needed to be placed before her eyes for her to see things as they really are.

Once I was playing paintball with some friends at a bachelor party when I was shot with a paintball in the face—hit directly in the goggles I was wearing. How thankful I was those goggles guarded my eyes. But with paint splattered across the plastic, I needed to remove those goggles entirely to see anything.

Sometimes in order to see life clearly we must add something to our lives—a new set of lenses to improve our vision. At other times we require a removal of some kind.

The disciplines of feasting and fasting can be seen in this way. There are times when our feasts need to be seen with new lenses—our delicious coffees or teas and foods need to be received with greater thanksgiving and contemplation. On the other hand, there will be times when we need to take things away in order to see God anew in our lives. Abstaining from food or technology might give us a vision of God that has been blurred because of our inability to remove the very things we've needed to all along.

I suppose the problem arises when we start to realize a secret about disciplines like prayer, fasting, feasting, and Scripture reading: the results are rarely seen immediately. And so we must go one level deeper together.

Chapter 10

TRUSTING/RELEASING

**My Lord God, I have no idea where
I am going . . . Therefore I will trust you always.**[1]
THOMAS MERTON

In a crowded classroom amidst the noise of eighth-grade bodies jostling to find their seats before the first bell rings, I hear my buddy Grant (not his real name) say my name.

"Dude, Chris."

"What?"

I had just returned from my very first church trip and had experienced what I believed to be God's presence in my life for the first time—I was just getting to know the Creator of Everything, and everything was getting seriously complicated in my middle-school brain.

Tired from a week away in the middle of nowhere, I was also wondering how that experience was going to change the life I was living and wanted to live. I really believed I had met with God on this trip and I was unsure of the consequences. My mind rattled with how it would all work out. I had this girlfriend at the time (whatever that means in eighth grade) and had a dream to get out of private school and be a public school kid where all the parties were happening and the dress code was loose. The mental tension broke when Grant started speaking again.

"My brother is throwing a party tonight and you need to be there," he says. Grant's older brother, Brandon, was the coolest person I knew when I was in the eighth grade. He drove a Pontiac Grand Prix and had seen Sublime in concert once. He wore what seemingly every Cool Kid Character wears in TV shows: an old army jacket and baggy pants. Brandon smoked cigarettes and had just turned seventeen, which meant every drag was filled with a single inspiring, illegal breath. I wanted to be like Brandon in nearly every way and, although I was scared to try cigarettes and had no idea how to drive a car, I thought I could pull it off. Brandon was the first person to show me bands like Phish and Violent Femmes, music I would spend seven years pretending to like. He and Grant were our private school's cultural connoisseurs and highbrow critics, explaining to me and my other friends why Pink Floyd mattered and what *A Clockwork Orange* was really all about (they turned out to be wrong about a lot of things).

That may explain to you, perhaps, why this party intrigued me. In eighth grade, the normal party for me and my friends involved eating a lot of Never-Ending-Gob-Stoppers, playing *Tony Hawk's Pro Skater* on PlayStation, and, sorry to say, watching a movie that had partial nudity in it. We were wild.

This, however, would be the next level. I remember imagining myself at Grant's house with a cigarette hanging out of my mouth nonchalantly agreeing with some hypothesis Brandon had about a Led Zeppelin record.

"Yeah," I would say, slightly nodding my head. "Sure, I can see that."

This was the life I dreamed for myself—it was my way out of the typical American life I had been brought up in and my way into the real stuff: music, laughter, sex, and a car. This is literally all any kid can imagine in middle school.

My daydreaming was interrupted when I thought about proposing any of this to my parents. They knew Brandon and they knew what he was about—or at least this was the impression I had. There was no way I could pitch this *and* get a ride out to their house nearly twenty minutes away.

"Dude," I said, "my parents would never let me. They know your brother."

And then Grant threw the dagger: "Mackenzie will be there."

Mackenzie went to public school and was, for whatever it means, the girlfriend I was "in a relationship with" before I left for the church trip. The party, the girl, and the best kids were the makings of a pure adolescent dream. It was all right before me.

But this was exactly the tension: what *was* my dream, exactly? What life did I really want to live? I had this one dream to be everything *I* wanted to be: chase girls, become famous, make money, and experience as much pleasure as possible and a minimal amount of suffering. But then there was the dream to be everything *God* wanted me to be and made me to be: to pray, to give my life to those less fortu-

> I had this one dream to be everything I wanted to be. Then there was the dream to be everything *God* wanted me to be. Something had to give.

nate than me, to be unbelievably generous with money and involved in people's lives, to truly care about them, sacrifice for them, and understand the person of Jesus more deeply. I really desired both dreams, but something had to give.

What do you do when your life *with* God competes against a life that *makes you like* a god? The exchange Adam and Eve made in the garden of Eden was that simple: they chose to be like God instead of with Him. I get caught in between this decision often—even as an adult.

I can remember this moment with my buddy Grant because it was the first of a thousand moments where I was not fully convinced that this life of acting and obeying within God's plan and presence would be worth it. The Christian life is a continuous process of offering the ideas we have about life to God and allowing Him to redefine them.

I also remember this exchange in the eighth grade because I remember the outcome—the perhaps unexpected and anticlimactic ending to the story: I broke up with the girl and didn't go to the party. And I remember this because it was one of the first times I trusted Jesus and His way.

Many Christians would say I "trusted Jesus" when I professed belief in Him at the camp I attended the week before this conversation with Grant, but I think I trusted Jesus when I began obeying Him and seeing His ways as better than my ways and reorienting my life in His favor.

This is part of understanding how to, as Brother Lawrence would say, "practice" the presence of God: trusting. There comes a point where we as Christians just need to keep doing the things we are certain God has commanded us to do over and over again. We need to trust that the ways of God are better than the ways of man and we cannot sway, but instead remain steadfast in our commitment to Him.

HE IS THE MASTER

"Jesus is the smartest man in the world."

Dallas Willard said this possibly a hundred times. (By now you can tell I'm a big Dallas Willard fan.) This comes from a section near the beginning of his best work and maybe one of the better books ever written, *The Divine Conspiracy*.[2] I often use this phrase in my own walk to be reminded to trust Him: Jesus is smarter than I am.

It may seem obvious and a bit juvenile, but consider it for a moment: every time we do not obey God, we are essentially saying we have a better idea about how to live than He does. When we harbor bitterness instead of letting forgiveness bloom, or tell lies or act spiritual so we can get attention, we announce our belief that we are smarter than God.

Jesus was the master at living a good life. He knew how to live well, maintain joy amidst adversity, and freely forgive the enemies He had in His life. Jesus was so free, so happy, and so secure that He could bless the very people who were publicly murdering Him (Luke 23:34). When I read the Gospels, I am astounded at Jesus' ability to live so freely. I want to live like Him and to take commands from the Person who lived the greatest life in human history. He was in constant communion with His Father, a master of prayer and patience, and someone people genuinely enjoyed being around. He commanded rooms with humble authority, stood His ground during times of testing and affliction, and gave great attention to the poor and marginalized. He was always near God. This is why we need to trust Jesus and be like Him. He lived a beautiful life . . . and we can too.

NOT DOING THE RIGHT THING

The issue we may all be thinking is a simple one: *it's not that easy*. Yes, the problem of trusting and obeying God—of practicing His presence daily—is not an issue of us *not knowing the right thing to do*. More often than not, we do know the right thing to do—we just do the opposite.

You know who else had this problem? The apostle Paul, who wrote most of the New Testament, including the famous letter to the Romans. In it, Paul has a striking statement: "For I know that nothing good dwells in me, that is, in my flesh. For I have the desire to do what is right, but not the ability to carry it out" (7:18). Sound familiar? *The desire to do what is right, but not the ability.*

Have you ever been here? You come home to your parents or your spouse after a difficult day and convince yourself you've earned time by yourself, alone in front of a TV with a nice beverage and a snack. The issue is, there are things that need to be done: dishes must be scrubbed or dinner must be prepared or trash must be taken out. You decide you've done good work all day and the members of your family should understand your need for "me time." But when Mom or your spouse asks for help and they seemingly don't understand your need for "me time," you snap at them. They walk away (or perhaps cower), you have time to zone out, and you are exactly where you want to be: alone and away from any possibility of relationships. You had a simple choice between service and selfishness, giving to others for the greater good or being greedy. You knew the right thing to do, but you lacked the ability to carry it out.

Or what about this: you wake up to your smartphone's alarm buzzing and vibrating on your nightstand. It is 6 a.m. Briefly, you look around your room to see the sun has not risen yet, and your motivation to get up wanes. Eventually you sluggishly move out of bed, freshen up, dress, and miraculously prepare some sad excuse for a breakfast. It's so early and you just need to zone out. You know you'll fall asleep reading your Bible or praying and so Twitter it is. The glow of your screen wakes you up and your day moves along without engaging with God. You had a simple choice between prayer and plugging in, seeking the face of God or the face of man. You knew the right thing to do, but you lacked the ability to carry it out.

Paul gives us the heart-wrenching picture of our battle between our knowledge and our abilities in Romans 7 to set up one of the most beautiful chapters in all of the Bible: Romans 8.

THE ABILITY TO DO THE RIGHT THING

In Romans 8, Paul tells us we have been set free (v. 2) to do what Christ has called us to do. "You . . . are not in the flesh," he writes (v. 9). Let's just sit with that for a second: you are not in the flesh; Jesus' work on the cross has made you born of the Spirit if you so choose to believe in His name (vv. 1–7). Now, Paul writes, you aren't in any flesh, "if in fact the Spirit of God dwells in you" (Romans 8:9b).

I love how he puts this: if you've got the Spirit, you've got the Spirit, and our flesh need not dominate us. This is the supernatural work that happens in a person who responds to the good news of Jesus. God dwells in you through His Holy Spirit. And this enables you and I to do the right thing.

Paul goes on to say, "If the Spirit of him who raised Jesus from the dead dwells in you, he who raised Christ Jesus from the dead will also give life to your mortal bodies through his Spirit who dwells in you" (v. 11).

Read that verse again.

Now, let me ask you this question: do you believe that? Or put a different way: do you trust this reality? Do you believe that God dwells in you through His Holy Spirit and will provide whatever you need to obey Him?

Life with the Spirit of God in us is not a perfect life, but it is a life that is being perfected. We are still able to sin, but, through the Spirit, we can obey God and have the ability to reject sin's temptation.

THE BEAUTY OF BEING PROVEN WRONG

So, when we know the right thing to do, but, as Paul says, don't have the ability to carry it out, we need to pause and remember who to rely on. The truth is, we don't have the ability to carry out the life of Jesus in our own lives, but God's Spirit does.

This is yet another connection between obedience and God's presence. When we trust Jesus and trust God's Spirit to help us obey, we are no longer doing this life by ourselves, but we're accepting the help we need and therefore building the relationship we need with our Father (vv. 12–17).

What happens next?

Well, the problem is that normally nothing happens next. After we disobey we normally go about our day just fine. These are tiny examples, but we all can think of larger ones. How easy is it to hide an addiction to pornography these days? Lies are not often noticed, are they? Being a gossip is actually a positive thing in our culture and being outraged seems to be all the rage. We do not often see the consequences of our disobedience.

But it always comes. Sin always pays us back, unfortunately (Rom. 6:23). Relationships are strained or broken, people are hurt, we become ashamed, we try and cover up the bad thing we seem to have made of our life, and before we know it, God feels very, very far away.

This is where I see most of us get stuck: we forget that a life of disobedience disconnects us from God and continually pays us back poorly. We are not living as happy of a

A life of disobedience disconnects us from God and continually pays us back poorly.

life as possible when we choose ways other than God's. God is right and we are wrong. What do we have to do to remind ourselves?

Try thinking through your life just for a second: have you ever regretted obeying God? I know often times I don't feel great *right away* about obeying God, but I know that as I look back on that busy eighth-grade classroom I don't regret giving up a Friday night—I probably would have been underwhelmed by the party.

I've discovered my life of faith is about Jesus slowly proving me wrong and Him right. When I first heard Jesus' teaching on loving your enemies, I agreed with it intellectually. Then someone betrayed me and spread lies about me. After that, I started to rethink Jesus' teachings and question His intentions. *How can this be the right thing to do right now? Pray for them? Now?* And through gritted teeth matched with white knuckles I trusted Jesus and began praying for them. Slowly, as I prayed, no circumstances changed, but I was proven wrong as forgiveness flooded my once bitter heart. Jesus proved Himself right: prayer and forgiveness are better than bitterness and resentment; it just takes a while to get there. The road is longer and the way is more difficult, but the life inside the obedience is more full of happiness.

A famous Proverb says, "Trust in the Lord with all your heart, and do not lean on your own understanding. In all your ways acknowledge him, and he will make straight your paths" (Prov. 3:5–6). Amen.

But, wait a second—what happens when that straight path God makes is also difficult and narrow?

Those verses in Proverbs are on coffee mugs and Instagram posts all over the world. When we read them, there is some comfort felt in our bones—God is good and He will make straight our paths. But then you have a moment like I had with my eighth grade pal Grant, when the way into a deeper knowledge of God and a life continually in His presence, on His path, is actually difficult.

One of the things I have gotten better at over the years is telling new Christians how difficult Christianity will be. It is not easy, but it is good. The way ahead may seem long at times, and it will certainly offer creative difficulties, but what if that same road filled with tough terrain led to a place of unimaginable joy? In part 3 we will look at that road that leads to joy.

GOING THE DISTANCE

EVERYONE HAS BEEN in a class they were waiting to end. Their eyes become fixed on the clock slowly changing, second by second, even as they begged it would speed up. *Is this really what a second feels like?* At times, life feels as long as that never-ending class.

When I was dating Ali, we spent most of our relationship living in different cities three hours away. I can remember driving up to see her one Friday afternoon, obsessively looking at the clock on the dusty dashboard as the miles flew by and the Northwest rain lightly dusted my windshield. The time seemed to drag by with unconscionable slowness and the more excited I got to see her, the more the clock seemed to stand still. I put my hand in my coat pocket to make sure the diamond ring was still there.

Pain and joy can do the same thing to time: slow it down. The seconds of life—both the good and bad—tick by with surprising reluctance, but the years fly by. The thing about life is not that it is short or long, but that it is temporary. Both the drudgery and the drive of everything remind us of life's fleeting nature. The quickness and slowness of time instructs us in the reality of each second's value. We must use it all well.

Time and life are the same. It's not about how long or short it is; it's about how you use however long or short it may be.

Chapter 11

THE ROAD

The process will be long and in parts very painful, but that is what we are in for. Nothing less. He meant what he said.[1]
C. S. LEWIS

My wife was at her discipleship group one night, probably making conversation over some type of delicious dessert because, well, women's ministry events always have the best food. She was talking with one of her mentors (so I heard) when the topic of me came up (how thrilling).

"Chris has like a hundred mentors," one of the women said.

My wife reported this story back to me in humor, but it's actually quite true. I have a lot of people older than me who I look to—I love it. These are men (for the most part) who have lived a lot of life very well. They're not perfect, but they've been obeying God for a long period of time. Eugene Peterson would say they possess "a long obedience in the same direction."[2] That's the type of guys

I follow. They have wonderful families, strong marriages, fulfilling jobs, stable homes, and tend to be very funny and extremely happy. I want to be like them.

Here's something I'm noticing that is similar about my "hundreds" of mentors. People think they got lucky. It's not uncommon for me to be talking with someone about one of my mentors and, as we are considering the awesomeness of their life, I'll hear someone remark, "Man, he's got a great deal . . . great wife and really good kids. That guy got lucky."

I am always uncomfortable when I hear this for one simple reason: they aren't just lucky. You see, what people don't understand is that life is all about choices and decisions—mostly small ones and then a couple of big ones.

My mentors are the guys they are today because of a long road of obedience where they have been practicing God's presence through times of ease and times of great trials. They have chosen what Jesus called "the narrow gate." "The gate is narrow," He says, "and the way is hard," but . . . it "leads to life" (Matt. 7:13–14).

When I see someone who has lived a full life before God, I do not think it has happened by accident. What interests me is not the particular circumstances of their past, but the tiny decisions they made along the way to become the man or woman they are now.

We know the consequences for our disobedience include various forms of decay and death. Life will not go well for us if we continue to chart our own path. However, have you ever thought about the consequences for your obedience? They are plentiful.

Imagine a life filled with the presence of God, a life where no death, divorce, or disease could rob your joy. Imagine being a person unafraid of anything —a person of courage and strength whom people come to. Can you fathom being regularly filled with happiness, free to forgive people who bulldoze you and try to take advantage of you? Can you think about not being intimidated by death?

These are some of the many wonderful consequences that come from obedience to God. It's also the kind of person Jesus was and the kind of life He imagines for you, but it can't be received without effort. This kind of life has never been bestowed on anyone. Rather, the vision for this kind of life is cast to all people everywhere. Jesus only calls to us: "*Strive* to enter through the narrow door" (Luke 13:24, emphasis added).

As we strive to enter this narrow gate by obeying Jesus through all of the ways we have described in this book, it is easy to see how much effort faith takes. There is a type of striving in this life with God. But just as the efforts will be plentiful, so will the rewards and benefits.

THE BENEFITS OF STAYING ON THE ROAD

When we begin this trusting obedience to Jesus, we need to trust Him for all of the benefits and blessings too. It can be tempting to desire and expect from God a spiritual pat on the back—a "well done, good and faithful servant" (Matt. 25:21)—after every small thing we do.

When I started ministry, I was startled to learn that the more leadership you get, the *less* thanks/pats-on-the-back you receive. This is because with more church leadership comes a lot more difficult, small work no one will ever see. Sure, the stage I preach on is bigger, but the difficult meetings and one-on-ones with staff members increase as well.

Early on, I would leave a tough meeting where I had to say things that were tough to say, but needed to be said. I would pray, seek wisdom, and then head in and speak the truth in love as best I could. Afterward, I would look around and no one was there to see my obedience. Nobody to tell me "well done" or tell me how inspired they were by my actions. Instead my actions seemed unnoticed to everyone.

Well, everyone but God. God is the one who always sees our obedience to Him and loves rewarding and providing those who follow and trust in His ways (2 Chron. 16:9, Ps. 1:1–6, Prov. 3:1–12, Matt. 7:24–27). Down the difficult path of discipleship, we must trust that God will provide for us what we need, when we need it, so long as we are living in step with His will. There certainly are benefits to this life, but they come at the most surprising times in the most unusual ways. The benefits of walking with God in His presence are real, but the timing can often be difficult. Life with God is often separate from the American life of instant gratification. Whenever we forget this, we must remember Abraham.

ABRAHAM'S LONG WALK UP THE MOUNTAIN

In perhaps his most famous moment, Abraham is tested by YHWH, the God of the Bible. God asks Abraham to take his only son, Isaac, up to the top of a mountain to kill him as a sacrificial offering to the Lord (Gen. 22:1–3).

My theological cohort in seminary—a small group of pastors and theologians—spent nearly an entire day on this passage, trying to understand how and why this story exists. It is totally crazy. We are still thinking about it.

But as you continue to read the Genesis 22 account, the story is breathtakingly beautiful. Abraham trusts God, takes his son with wood and knife, and heads up the trail to the top of the hill. Sometimes this is life with God: doing things and carrying things just because God told you to— no other reason. You find yourself traveling down a dusty road, tired and confused, half-thinking everything will be OK . . . and also half-convinced none of this makes sense.

As they walk up the road to the top of the hill I can imagine the piercing and awkward silence. The text hints at this. "My father," Isaac says, "the fire and the wood [are here], but where is the lamb for a burnt offering?" (v. 7). Great question, Isaac: where *is* the lamb? We seem to have everything here but a sacrifice.

Abraham's reply is perfect: "God will provide for himself the lamb."

Did Abraham know he wouldn't be killing his only son that day? I don't know. But it seems to me that no matter what he knew, he was certain God would provide. He knew God would meet him *at some point* along the terrifying and uncertain path of obedience. If God commanded this, the result would be good.

And it was. At the final moment, after he ties his son to the stones and splinters from the wood push up against

Isaac's back, Abraham raises a knife above the boy's throat. Suddenly, God steps in through an angel who stops the scene: "Do not lay your hand on the boy or do anything to him, for now I know that you fear God" (v. 12). And then, "behind him was a ram, caught in a thicket by his horns" (v. 13). God had provided.

LONGER THAN WE MIGHT EXPECT

I often want instant rewards for my smallest obedience—the same way I want to put off any bad consequences for my largest disobedience. The thing is, I've noticed our selfishness catches up to us more quickly than our selflessness. What I mean is, you will often reap the bad things that come from a bad decision faster than the good things that come from a good decision. And one of those good rewards is God's full presence.

When I do the right thing and follow God in a specific moment, I do not get a rush of the Holy Spirit in my life all of the time. I tell a lot of students this when they're beginning a daily devotional life in the Scriptures. Every day will not be mind-blowingly rewarding. In fact, most days will be boring and difficult. But as we obey and trust God down the narrow road, one of those inspiring moments with the risen Jesus is coming. It will happen; God will provide.

I cannot tell you how many times I have been surprised at how God provides His presence in my life. Randomly (it seems), I will be reading Scripture or praying (as I do nearly every day) or even preaching or leading a Bible study and teaching God's Word, when all of a sudden the Holy Spirit comes very near to me. I can never control it or expect it, but I keep my eyes fixed on the goal, knowing God will provide everything I need when I need it. Sometimes that has come with financial benefit, other times it has come with deep spiritual peace, or the presence of a godly friend when I needed that friend most. You will never know all of the consequences for your obedience, but I promise they will come at some point and they will always be wonderful.

Do you think Abraham felt close to God when he heard that voice and saw that ram caught in the thicket? I can't help but think so. But do you think Abraham *felt* close to God when he was walking up that silent path to the top of the hill, preparing his mind for the unbelievable task of offering his son as a sacrifice, before a God he had never seen? I can't help but think he did not. Even though he knew intellectually God would provide, Abraham likely felt fear and uncertainty. That's our struggle as well, between knowing and feeling.

Part of trusting God in the long run is realizing life can sometimes feel like a long run. We're not in the 100-meter sprint; we're in the marathon. There will be times of great struggle, thinking God is out to get us, wondering as the psalmist has wondered, "Why, O Lord, do you stand far away? Why do you hide yourself in times of trouble" (Ps. 10:1)? We must know that for every verse and time in our life like this one, there are also times when we can't help but exclaim, "You make known to me the path of life; in your presence there is fullness of joy; at your right hand are pleasures forevermore" (Ps. 16:11). Our job is to keep walking, keep trusting.

JUST LIKE THE MENTORS

Even though I get uncomfortable when I hear people talk about my mentors saying, "they got lucky," there's a part of me hoping someone might say that about me one day. My wife and I desire a full family, one able to withstand storms and troubles, a life filled with the Holy Spirit and generous to those who are in need of anything. I can see this life because I see it in the homes of those we look up to.

But I don't just sit with wishful thinking, because I realize no one stumbles into a godly life. Christlikeness is no accident and a life filled with God's Holy Spirit presence is not something people fall into. Instead, it requires long-term, sacrificial commitment to believing God has for me the things He has promised. I have not arrived, but I just want to take the next step, knowing the way can be long and the gate can be narrow.

As I look at the lives of the people I admire and wish to be like, I notice they have not had lives absent of difficulty, but ones filled with it. Strange as it may seem, people who live with strength and perseverance are like Abraham. They understand how difficult life can be. The only difference is they also understand life to be even more difficult if they were to do it without God's guiding presence.

I guess the difference can be seen in these guys when you hear they have lost jobs, dreams, spouses, and homes, but when they talk about it, they talk about how God brought them through, how He fought for them and protected them, even though the opposition seemed impossible to fight.

Chapter 12

THE DEFENSE

Obviously you are making excellent progress.[1]
SCREWTAPE TO WORMWOOD (C. S. LEWIS)

I quit football in the eighth grade for two very predictable reasons. The first reason was that I was terrible at football. The second involved the unmistakable fact that the other players on my team and the other teams got much bigger while I stayed the same, small size through most of adolescence.

This didn't stop my love for football, particularly college football. And it was sometime during my freshman year of college when I heard a metaphor about football and faith that really connected with me. I can't remember who shared it, but I know I didn't make it up, because, as I said, I am terrible at football.

Imagine a running back breaking free of the first line of defense and beginning to make progress down the field toward the end zone. He hasn't been touched and he can see a path laid before him ending in a touchdown. But, as he goes fifteen yards past the line of scrimmage, out of nowhere, a large linebacker blindsides him, tackling him to the ground (this is common in football).

But now imagine, upon getting up after the play is dead, the running back who had the ball throws it to the ground and begins pouting.

"Hey!" he yells at the linebacker. "Why did you do that? I didn't like when you tackled me! What were you doing?"

Everyone on the field and in the stands would be flabbergasted, right? We would be so confused because it would be as if the running back had no idea what game he was playing. An essential part of football is defense, and getting tackled happens more often than not getting tackled. This is a perfectly normal part of the game.

Unfortunately, many Christians feel surprised when life, with its temptation, suffering, or setbacks, throws them to the turf. When we get knocked down in our faith life, our first response tends to be, "Why is this happening?" But what if we had a better understanding of the game? Getting tackled is perfectly normal and should be expected. We must be better prepared.

SURPRISED

When we read our Bibles, we can see its pages are bloody. The Scriptures do not avoid suffering and trouble or show us how to work around it; rather, the writers of the Bible include suffering everywhere. The pastor and apostle Paul tells his protégé Timothy, "All who desire to live a godly life in Christ Jesus will be persecuted" (2 Tim. 3:12). Jesus tells His followers, "In this world you will have trouble" (John 16:33 NIV). "The Bible, therefore, is about suffering as much as it is about anything."[2] Our Bibles are very comfortable interacting with the difficult aspects of life.

As Americans, it is our goal to experience the most amount of pleasure and the least amount of suffering. We want a life that does not include difficult things. If we accomplish this, we are winners and admired. But what if the suffering we try to avoid would actually shape us into more humble and helping people?

God's Word tells believers that life is difficult and dangerous, that the earth is a place filled with trouble. "Beloved," Peter tells early Christian communities, "do not be surprised at the fiery trial when it comes upon you to test you, as though something strange were happening to you" (1 Peter 4:12). He then tells them what James will tell Christians and we must tell each other now: don't be surprised, but rejoice (v. 13; cf. James 1:2).

In America, suffering is surprising; in the Bible, it is assumed. Even Christians today are committed to creating a life with the least amount of suffering possible. We believe if we surround ourselves with enough money and possessions, and if we're good people, we will evade most suffering. This quasi-karma leads us to be distraught when even the smallest amount of spiritual depression seeps in. When unexpected sickness happens, a new temptation surfaces, or a relationship begins to wither, we think, *How could this happen to us?*

When we talk about "God's promises" in our lives, we forget one of them is about suffering, temptations, and trials. "Do not be surprised," Peter warns us. We are guaranteed to face difficulties of many varieties. Why are we shocked when our life of faith is tested and we experience moments of drought?

THE TARGET ON YOUR BACK

I got started in ministry when I was eighteen by inviting sixty-five of my friends to a Bible study I would teach in my house. Five people came—most of them were my best friends who took pity on me. But, that little Bible study grew to one hundred people in its first year and I was amazed. People were getting baptized, breaking up unhealthy relationships, even selling possessions—and, in the midst of it all, I had no idea what I was doing.

During this early season of ministry, I found myself at lunch with one of my church's elders with a solid portion of chips and salsa separating us. He was being very complimentary to my ministry and we were celebrating the things God was doing. The tone was light and the festive colors in this particular Mexican restaurant added to the delight. As the conversation found one of its lulls, the church elder changed his tone. He wiped his mouth with the teal napkin and looked at me for a brief second.

"So, Chris, things are going well and I want you to know I'm so proud of you. But you need to know something."

"Yeah?" I said.

"You've been successful, God is using you, people are looking to you as a leader now, and that's a great thing. But it also means this: you have a target on your back now."

I took a big drink of my iced tea and didn't say anything.

"Imagine you're in a war . . . think Normandy or something, storming a beach with a huge army around you," he said. "If you were in that war and saw a wounded enemy soldier bleeding out and nearly dead, are you going to pay attention to him and try to kill him?"

"I don't think so," I said. I have very limited knowledge of combat, but was trying my best to act confidently.

"You wouldn't," he said. "You're going after the guy who's upright, strong, and making an impact." He paused for a second. "Satan works the same way. If he can take you down, he knows he can always take a lot of other people down too. That's what has changed. I know you've got growth in ministry and amazing things happening, but remember, Chris: there is an enemy, there is defense, and you need to be prepared."

This particular elder had tons of ministry experience; he loved me and loves Jesus. This is what wise people do sometimes: they encourage you at the same time they warn you.

I have lived in the great reality of this reminder and am forever grateful for this man's word into my life. So many Christians live unaware of the defense, unable to understand the devil's schemes, but Scripture warns about it often (e.g., Eph. 6:11; 1 Peter 5:8) and somewhat normalizes it. This is just part of the game.

There are so many ways I could approach the enemy and his ways, but for our subject at hand—the presence of God and our awareness of it—I think about two broad categories I see as the winds that cause people to drift away from God: trials and temptations.

HOW WE DRIFT FROM GOD: TRIALS

"In this world you will have trouble," Jesus said (John 16:33. Do you believe this promise of His? You need not live long to have seen this promise fulfilled in your own life. Maybe it was through a relationship that ended with betrayal and pain, or an illness crippling you or a loved one, or maybe someone very close to you passed away. These are all trials.

Trials are normally the terrible things that happen outside of our control. We are surprised by them, hurt by them, and overwhelmed as we wonder how we might move on. Trials are moments when we question if God really knows what He's doing. When these questions and doubts arise, our primary mistake—and the one I believe takes us out of the presence of God—is when we choose not to interact with Him in the midst of it all.

What I mean is, when the terrible things happen in this life, often we run *from* God and not *to* Him. Then, after we've never told Him how we feel or what we're thinking, we blame Him for going away. We wonder why God would leave us, but we never wonder why we would leave God. We think too highly of ourselves.

> When doubts arise, our primary mistake is when we choose not to interact with God.

Next time you are caught in the unimaginable or the understandable-but-still-difficult stuff of life, run *to* God. "Seek first the kingdom of heaven," Jesus tells us. It's OK to take our hurt, our pain, and our mistrust to God Himself. Let Him take it; He can handle it. Enter into His presence, seek His Spirit, and speak to Him all of your worries. Peter tells early Christians to put "all your anxieties on him, because he cares for you" (1 Pet. 5:7). *All* of them.

Tell God you're having trouble trusting Him.

Tell Him you think He could do more.

Tell Him you don't see a purpose or a way forward.

When you and I don't do this—when we go silent before God—we allow the trials to win, to own us and control us. Before we know it, we start telling our friends about how God wasn't there for us. But all the while He *was* there for us, we just decided not to speak to Him.

"The Lord is near to the brokenhearted," says David (Ps. 34:18). God is always in the rooms of suffering; we just fail to acknowledge His presence. Putting our problems on God's shoulders requires us to be *with* Him, which is what we were created for. When we ignore God during times of suffering and try to handle everything on our own, we should not be surprised when we feel distant from Him weeks later.

HOW WE DRIFT FROM GOD: TEMPTATIONS

If you want an example of the presence of God in a close, intimate, manifest way, look at the baptism of Jesus in Luke 3:21–22. God's Spirit descends "like a dove" and a voice comes from heaven to bless the work, ministry, and personhood of Jesus the Messiah. It is epic.

Do you know what happens after this transcendent experience with the presence of God? Luke tells us, "And Jesus, full of the Holy Spirit, returned from the Jordan and was led by the Spirit in the wilderness for forty days, being tempted by the devil" (Luke 4:1–2).

Jesus was baptized, experienced the Holy Spirit's power and the love of His Father in a glorious way, and then was *led by that same Spirit* to be tempted by the devil himself for forty days. I always warn my students after a missions trip or a camp: the defense is coming, temptations are coming, the target on our backs is growing. Get ready.

It is not uncommon for one of my students to follow up a great season of closeness to God with a rough season of distance and confusion. I can remember Marcus, a young guy in my youth group, who had never really had a ton of success with girls before he was a Christian.

"After I came to Christ, it was like the ladies were throwing themselves at me—what's with that?" He said this to me one afternoon at a Starbucks. Marcus recognized this as temptation, and was really surprised by the timing of it.

It's a funny thing, but temptations seem to come after we profess faith so that God can test the faith we profess. In Scripture, temptations are never given by God, but they are allowed by Him (James 1:13–15). We are promised blessing if we withstand temptations (James 1:12). Nevertheless, temptation shows up in our lives to prove its truth: that blessings may come as the temptation allows us the chance to trust God and release power back to where it belongs. If we come through to the other side having stood the test, we will find a reward because we will be with God Himself in a renewed closeness.

I need to mention something now that is not always

obvious to Christians: *being tempted is not a sin.* Jesus was tempted and never sinned (Heb. 4:15). Many Christians sense temptation and think they've already failed, but they haven't—they're just on the verge of success and blessing if they withstand. Temptation is something we can and should withstand, knowing God is allowing it to make us right before Him and grow in our relationship with Him. We do not need to be dismayed, but rather know God has us and will protect us through our trials *and* temptations— He will provide a way out and a possibility for victory (1 Cor. 10:13).

GOD WILL NOT ALWAYS SEEM NEAR

My friend Andrew tells this amazing story about rafting in a California river when he was in college. During the brief training session before Andrew went out rafting, he was told that if he ever fell out of the boat, he should rely on his lifejacket, lift his legs, and become a ball so he could float to the top of the river and not be caught in any undercurrents and drown. This frightened Andrew.

In the middle of the trip, flying through top-class rapids, Andrew falls out of the raft. In a panic, Andrew becomes a ball and panics, screaming to his friend (a more experienced rafter) for help.

"Save meeeee!" Andrew yells. The water is moving quickly and he is becoming more desperate.

"Dude," his friend says. "Stand up."

What Andrew didn't realize was he was "drowning" in three feet of water.

Notice Andrew did not trust the instructions. He became that floating ball on the surface of the rapids but did not believe it would help. Eventually it would not matter, thanks to the water's depth. But he forgot the deliverance already provided after he assumed the ball position. In addition, he did not think that God could provide. Yet God is near when we call and often is involved when we don't—that's called grace. God had provided. Even though Andrew *felt* like he was drowning in the deep currents, the truth is he never had the possibility of drowning. God had Andrew bob furiously—but over shallow waters. The churning waters made him think it was deep, but it was actually shallow.

I love this story because it reminds me how *what we feel is often very different from what is true*. A lot of our faith life is reminding ourselves of the truth in spite of how we're feeling.

There will be times in your life when God does not *feel* near, when you sense waters of life to be deep and frightening. Through temptation and trial, you may think the day of death is near, but no matter. God *is* near to you, God *is* available—*He does hear your prayers*. Stay persistent, preach to yourself, and continue to pray—now is not the time to give up! Trials and temptations and "the flaming darts of the evil one" are certain to come your way, but the truth is that with the power of the Holy Spirit you will never drown, and the water is not as deep as you think it is.

Remember the famous words of Psalm 23, "Even though I walk through the valley of the shadow of death, I will fear no evil, for *you are with me*" (Ps. 23:4, emphasis added).

God is with you and most likely at work even—and maybe more so—when the sunshine of life is blocked by the looming shadow of death. We often believe God has abandoned us during these seasons, but He is actually more present than we can imagine.

> There will be times when God does not *feel* near. But God *is* near to you—*He does hear your prayers*. Stay persistent.

A. J. Swoboda, a pastor, professor, and friend, wrote this line I quickly memorized because it is so true: "The hardest time to see God working in someone's life is that very moment when God is actually working in someone's life."[3] When the difficult things in life surround us, we are often certain God is not working because we don't *feel* His work. We may sense the enemy at work or the plans of evil people laboring against us. These are the seasons when people sit in my office *convinced* God is distant from them. I have been learning these are the times He is most intimately at work—trying our faith and testing us so we might prove to be worthy of the rewards He so earnestly desires to give us.

KNOWING AND PREPARING

It helps me to know that I will not always feel near to God. I am reassured when I remember that God's relational presence comes into and out of my life sometimes. Yet the Holy Spirit remains (John 14:16–17; Acts 2:38), though we may stifle the Spirit's work in us (Eph. 4:30).

Just *knowing* a defense exists helps us prepare for every day and inspires us to pray and ask God to "deliver us from evil" (Matt. 6:13). For us to think the Christian life will offer no trial or temptation is to ignore very large portions of Scripture and forget one of the primary identities of the early church. Thus, we need "not be surprised when the fiery trial comes" (1 Pet. 4:12).

But it also is a great truth that Jesus will be "with you always, to the end of the age" (Matt. 28:20). His general presence and Holy Spirit dwells in me and around me—"Where shall I go from your Spirit" (Ps. 139:7)? When we know these things, we are better prepared. We are not playing a game without defense, but on our team is the greatest offense in all of history. Matched with the promise that we will have trouble is the promise that we will have victory: "In this world you will have trouble," Jesus says. "But take heart! I have overcome the world" (John 16:33 NIV). We will not perish or suffer forever. We will win.

Chapter 13

THE PROMISE

**A little faith will bring your soul to heaven;
a great faith will bring heaven to your soul.**[1]
CHARLES SPURGEON

Past the bustling main drag of candy stores, taverns, and gift shops along the Oregon coast town Cannon Beach, by the small city's limits, there is a cabin.

My mom and her husband have been renovating for the past year, retiling the bathroom and painting the walls for future guests to enjoy a secluded, Internet-free retreat surrounded by the sounds of falling waves and clean breezes. I am one of the first visitors.

Handling the steering wheel with one hand, I look in the backseat to check on my only passenger, our three-year-old dog, Zo. I am at peace. Not because I'm at the beach house yet, but because I'm headed there. I know I will arrive shortly, where I will be unable to respond to the various anxieties of ministry constantly swirling about in my head—and that is a good thing.

As I drive west along the winding coastal highways, I

am reminded of the way one seminary professor has talked about the Christian, kingdom-minded life: "already, but not yet."

Faith in Jesus is like driving to the cabin at the beach: I have peace now in the car driving with my dog, but I'm not there yet. I am receiving the peace that awaits me, even though I haven't arrived completely.

THINKING ABOUT HEAVEN

"My Father's house, has many rooms," Jesus tells His disciples. "I am going there to prepare a place for you" (John 14:2 NIV). He is renovating homes and clearing real estate for those who love Him. The cabins are being prepared, we are headed there, but it is clear based on the curving roads that the pleasant coastal breezes are not as near as we would like. Nevertheless, peace floods our hearts because we know, in a matter of time, *we will be there*—where God the Father and God the Son await.

I used to hate thinking about heaven for most of the reasons you may as well. I used to be afraid of Jesus returning or of death, because I wanted to live my life here on earth. I wanted girlfriends, money, people laughing at my jokes, plenty of travel experiences, and maybe a boat. But the more I live the more I resonate with some of Scripture's final words: "Come, Lord Jesus!" (Rev. 22:20).

The story your Bible tells ends in a wonderful place, and the story of every individual Christian life ends there too. We are promised to be surrounded by God entirely—all of us wrapped up in all of Him. There will be no end to

Him, but the entirety of our space will be enveloped in the completeness of Him. "Beloved," John writes to his churches, "we are God's children now, and what we will be has not yet appeared; but we know that when he appears we shall be like him, because we shall see him as he is" (1 John 3:2).

> We know just a little bit about heaven. But there is one thing certain . . . God will be there.

Heaven is a real place we know just a little bit about. But there is one thing certain about the heaven we will find either when we die or when Jesus returns for us: God will be there.

"Behold," exclaims John in Revelation as he sees the final day when God makes all things new and right, *the dwelling place of God is with man. He will dwell with them, and they will be his people, and God himself will be with them as their God*" (Rev. 21:3, emphasis added).

Every limitation you have ever had with God's presence will vanish on this day. Every moment you have cried, "Where are you?" will disappear into the instant light from the immense flames of His heavenly glory (Rev. 1:14–15; 4:5). This day *will happen*—we are promised by the same God who said, "You will have trouble" that we will also dwell with Him forever.

When members of the early church went through unimaginable suffering and persecution, they reminded one another of the day Jesus would return to make all things new—when tears would go away, when the plagues would be just a chapter in history and death would be deleted from life forever. "Encourage one another with these words," Paul told the Thessalonians after writing about the coming of the Lord (1 Thess. 4:18).

There are times we need to put the house Jesus is preparing for us at the forefront of our minds to make the delayed journey there more bearable. When we think on this day, it should bring us the peaceful presence of Christ, even though we are not with Him fully. I have never met a Christian who was "too heavenly minded." To be mindful of heaven is to be a Christian. To think about eternity and its riches is what it means to be able to do all the things we must do here on earth.

If all of the words of this book fail to encourage you, may Revelation 21 and 22 bring you a kind of peace, for God will one day make all things right, and if there is any comfort or consolation for us as we struggle wondering if God is real, near, or present, we must look toward heaven and its return to earth one day. We, there, in the fullness of God's holy presence, will never regret prayer, nor will we question our obedience or generosity. No. We will instead wish we would have pressed in further, prayed harder, suffered more for the gospel, because we will recognize what Jesus saw perfectly: it's all worth it (Heb. 12:1–2).

VICTORY IS OURS

"I will build my church," Jesus tells His disciples in Matthew 16:18, "and the gates of hell shall not prevail against it." It was pointed out to me very early on in faith that the gates are on hell, not on the church. In other words, we are not on the defensive, we're on the offensive. We're pushing forward, deleting oppression, and executing justice—that's us. Hell is the one placed into a corner, contained to the outskirts of town, and God will bulldoze all evil one day. God is certain to have victory and Jesus was sure of it. Are we as sure as Jesus?

I once heard the New Testament scholar Richard Hays speak in Seattle. I don't remember everything he said, but one line still stands out: "The book of Acts does not use the word, 'love,' once," he said. "This is because the book of Acts is not about love, but power."[2]

That line (and much of Hays' writings) has helped my view of Acts. When the church is beginning and Jesus is commissioning the apostles, He tells them, "You will receive power when the Holy Spirit has come upon you" (Acts 1:8). I don't tell new converts this enough, but when we become Christians and the Holy Spirit dwells within us, we become very powerful human beings.

There is a kind of confidence—a swagger, if you will—found in the apostles that matches the courage of Old Testament characters like David. They *knew* God would come through. These men and women were certain God would provide for them the things they needed, even if it didn't feel like it.

There's this remarkable line in the book of Hebrews I'm thinking about as I write this. "But recall the former days when, after you were enlightened, you endured a hard struggle with sufferings . . . and you joyfully accepted the plundering of your property, since you knew that you yourselves had a better possession and an abiding one" (10:32, 34).

What is the abiding possession other than the kingdom of God and God Himself? When we have God, His promises, and His kingdom, and we are working on their behalf and serving Him faithfully, Scripture seems to indicate we should not need anything else. And here's what is remarkable: our houses can be taken, our jobs can be lost, friend groups can change, and sickness may happen, but we can remain faithful.

The passage ends like this: "Therefore do not throw away your confidence. . . . For you have need of endurance, so that when you have done the will of God you may receive what is promised" (vv. 35–36).

WHEN THINGS WILL BE AS THEY SHOULD BE

This book began with an acknowledgment of God's distance, of our difficulty in closing the gap between Him and us. Because of sin, things are not as they should be. But just as we hold up this truth, we must hold up with absolute assurance the truth that one day things will be as they should be. Yes, things are not as they should be, but one day they will be.

Our whole lives are spent agonizing—groaning, even—at the inability to be fully human. We are depressed, anxious, and dissatisfied with the pleasures life gives us. Even our spiritual experiences with God seem to leave us wanting more. We are perpetually falling short from a vision of life we seem to have placed within us somewhere. It seems we live inside of a world where we cannot get enough. Nothing forever satisfies.

188

GETTING INTO HEAVEN

Our trust in Jesus leads us to look ahead—to look toward a day when all things will be as they should be and we will be united with all of the beauty we desire. In C. S. Lewis's greatest sermon (and one of his only sermons), he perfectly articulates this truth:

> We do not want merely to *see* beauty, though, God knows, even that is bounty enough. We want something else which can hardly be put into words—to be united with the beauty we see, to pass into it, to receive it into ourselves, to bathe in it, to become part of it... At present we are on the outside of the world, the wrong side of the door. We discern the freshness and purity of morning, but they do not make us fresh and pure. We cannot mingle with the splendours we see. But all the leaves of the New Testament are rustling with the rumour that it will not always be so. Some day, God willing, we shall get *in*.[3]

Heaven is precisely this—a way in. Even in life's most important moments, you have not been satisfied. Your desire is my desire: to be united and whole again. This is the life God has promised for us—a life we get to taste now and experience in full when we see God face-to-face. As we grow in life with God in His presence, we get hints of heaven, peeks behind the curtain until the day we receive the vision all at once.

Do you want to receive what is promised? Do you

desire heaven? Do you want life with God forever? There is a defense, but we must have confidence in the offense we are a part of. We must be certain that Jesus wins in the end, that the vision of the new heavens and the new earth found in Revelation is not some wish, but a reality.

There is, then, a glaring invitation in all of this. Those who desire the heavenly presence of God forever have it available to them now through the person and work of Jesus. The gospel writer John writes in his prologue to the story, "And the Word became flesh and dwelt among us, and . . . from his fullness we have all received, grace upon grace. . . . The only God, who is at the Father's side, he has made him known" (John 1:14, 16, 18).

I meet a lot of people who tell me they would believe in heaven and God if God would just show up. Well, I usually tell them, what if He already has?

Jesus Christ is God. He is heaven come to earth and He has given us an invitation. This invitation is not about getting to heaven later—it's about getting there now through Christ.

You may be reading this book and thinking *I am a Christian and bound for heaven.* If so, it is not because you were raised in the church or do good deeds, or say a prayer before every meal you eat. The question is, do you believe Jesus is the Son of God, sent to earth as the redeemer who sacrificed Himself for your sins? Have you received Him as Savior? If not, you can do so now. When we acknowledge this reality, we receive His grace, His forgiveness, His Holy Spirit, and His new heavenly life. We, because of faith in Christ, receive not only His presence, but everything else thrown in: happiness, comfort, guidance, prayer, life, peace, help, and compassion.

WHAT ABOUT OTHER RELIGIONS?

I once heard a teacher of mine talk about different religions as different paths up the same mountain. At the top of the mountain, he explained, sits God. To get to the top, there are many paths and trails. One might take the Buddhist approach; another may take the Mormon route or the Christian route. Nevertheless, he assured my class, all find their way to God. Maybe as a reader you feel this way.

I don't see this story in Scripture. In fact, I see the opposite. I see a God on a Holy Hill—a mountain no one can ascend (Psalm 24:3). We have blazed our own trails, cut through the brush, only to find ourselves lost in the mountain's terrifying realities. We do our good religious works only to continue to feel shame. We think through our most elaborate philosophies only to lack peace and continue to generate confusion. There's no way up this mountain—I've never met someone who has ascended to the top the way my professor described it.

Instead, the Christian story tells not of man climbing up the mountain to God, but God climbing down the mountain to man. This is the good news of Jesus. We do not climb aimlessly. Instead, God came down the mountain through Jesus, and He puts us on His back and carries us up. Jesus does not come down just to show us the way; *He is the way* (John 14:5–14). The story of Scripture is better than the story of religious tradition and philosophy.

It shows us the story of a God who loves His world so much, He didn't expect us to climb to the heavens. Instead, He brought them to us: "The kingdom of God is at hand!" Jesus proclaims at the start of His ministry (Mark 1:15). You do not need to frantically run about trying to prove yourself to this God and arrange for a way up the mountain to its peak. He has come down to find you. The access we desire to the presence that will heal us is fully accessible as we turn our attention toward Him and do exactly what the New Testament tells us to: receive.

As you and I receive this remarkable truth and stare heaven in the face while we're still on earth, everything changes. As the love of God is made clear and the Holy Spirit begins inhabiting our minds and hearts, we will find ourselves doing different things, practicing new habits. All of a sudden, we'll be acting like we're in heaven, but the strange thing is, we'll still be on earth.

Christians need not worry about a God who is far away on top of an unreachable mountain. He's already come. He's here. We now must trust Him and follow His lead. This Jesus is taking us somewhere no one could ever go alone: to the very dwelling place of God.

Certainly the challengers to a fully abundant life in God's presence will be many, but we must always remember the truth: *God is with us, God is for us.* In Jesus Christ, He became "Immanuel," and through His Holy Spirit He dwells in you now. A victory is coming, a reward is near— stand fast and persevere with confidence knowing these things to be truer than anything else in all of creation's past, present, and future.

NOTES

Chapter 1: The Longing to Be Near

1. Studies on evangelical experience and the brain are wide ranging and often repeated by multiple research groups and universities. The most comprehensive evaluation and summary of these studies for a popular reading audience can be found in T. M. Luhrmann, *When God Talks Back: Understanding the American Evangelical Relationship with God* (New York: Random House, 2012), particularly chapters 2 and 5.
2. Dallas Willard, *The Divine Conspiracy: Rediscovering Our Hidden Life In God* (New York: HarperOne, 1997), 61.
3. Stephen's address to the religious council and the high priest is marked by courage, especially his condemning words in 7:51–56.
4. In Paul's mind and in the understanding of the early church, the Holy Spirit was involved in the decisions churches made. The Spirit opened doors for them (2 Cor. 2:12–13) and instructed them in disagreements (Acts 15:28) as well as was an active part of worship services (1 Cor. 12–14). When Paul tells his congregation in Thessalonica to not "quench the Spirit" in conjunction with not "despising prophecies," he *is* referring to being careful in responding to God's revelation. This is why Paul tells them to "test everything."
5. Blaise Pascal, *Pensees*, #425, as cited in "Types of Apologetics," *The Popular Encyclopedia of Apologetics*, Ed Hinson and Ergun Caner, gen. eds. (Eugene, OR: Harvest House, 2008), 64.

Chapter 3: Finding Out Where You Are

1. Cornelius Plantinga Jr., *Not the Way It's Supposed to Be: A Breviary of Sin* (Grand Rapids: Eerdmans, 1995), 5.

Chapter 4: Adjusting Our Expectations

1. A.W. Tozer, *The Knowledge of the Holy* (New York: HarperCollins, 1961), 74.
2. Thomas Goodwin, a seventeenth-century Puritan pastor, wrote about an example similar to this. His example is cited in Timothy Keller, *Prayer: Experiencing Awe and Intimacy with God* (New York: Dutton, 2014), 172.
3. Dallas Willard, *The Divine Conspiracy: Rediscovering Our Hidden Life In God* (New York: HarperOne, 1997), 61.

4. Stephen J. Nichols, "The Deity of Christ Today," in *The Deity of Christ*, ed. Christopher W. Morgan & Robert A. Peterson et al. (Wheaton, IL: Crossway, 2011), 28.
5. J. Ryan Lister, *The Presence of God* (Wheaton, IL: Crossway, 2014), 65.
6. "Brother Lawrence Biography," www.thepracticeofthepresenceof god.com
7. Brother Lawrence, *The Practice of the Presence of God* (New Kensington, PA: Whitaker House, 1982), 67.

Chapter 5: Abiding/Obeying

1. Rich Mullins, from live concert footage at Lufkin, Texas, uploaded March 24, 2007, accessed on YouTube at the 5:30 mark: https://www.youtube.com/watch?v=vQnFU5JvuWY
2. Timothy Keller, *Walking with God through Pain and Suffering* (New York: Dutton, 2013), 5.
3. Robert E. Coleman, *The Mind of the Master* (Wilmore, KY: Christian Outreach, 2000), 44–45.
4. John 5:19; 12:49.
5. Dallas Willard, *Hearing God: Developing a Conversational Relationship with God* (Downers Grove, IL: InterVarsity, 2012), 61.
6. The short video can be accessed at https://www.youtube.com/wat ch?v=6wAcI1zY1jI&index=5&list=PLobCCMfoLPpYsMpIfkVL T5yLo3xWsGPi. McGinn is professor emeritus of the University of Chicago Divinity School.

Chapter 6: Praying/Listening

1. St. Gregory, as quoted in: Thomas Merton, *Contemplative Prayer* (New York: Image, 1996), 38.
2. Dietrich Bonhoeffer, *Psalms: The Prayer Book of the Bible* (Minneapolis: Augsburg Fortress, 1970), 15.
3. Learning to speak God's language so we can answer God is the premise of Peterson's book *Answering God: The Psalms As Tools for Prayer* (New York: HarperOne, 1984).
4. Dietrich Bonhoeffer, *Meditating on the Word* (Plymouth, UK: Roman & Littlefield Publishers, 2000), 31.
5. Timothy Keller, *Prayer: Experiencing Awe and Intimacy with God* (New York: Dutton, 2014), 93–94.
6. Interview with Dallas Willard posted August 18, 2011 at https://www.youtube.com/watch?v=GqLmeubS65Q

Chapter 7: Confessing/Repenting

1. Henri Nouwen, *In the Name of Jesus: Reflections on Christian Leadership* (New York: Crossroad Publishing, 1989), 20–21.

2. Dietrich Bonhoeffer, *Life Together* (New York: HarperCollins, 1954), 110.

Chapter 8: Preaching/Receiving

1. John Piper, *When I Don't Desire God: How to Fight for Joy* (Wheaton, IL: Crossway, 2004), 78–82.

Chapter 9: Feasting/Fasting

1. Ignatius of Loyola, *The Spiritual Exercises*, n. p.
2. A great and balanced summary of this teaching from Ignatius can be found in a wonderful modern book by Fr. James Martin, *The Jesuit Guide to Almost Everything* (New York: HarperOne, 2010).
3. Dallas Willard, *The Spirit of the Disciplines* (New York: HarperOne, 1991), 166.

Chapter 10: Trusting/Releasing

1. Thomas Merton, *Thoughts in Solitude* (repr., New York: Farrar, Straus, Giroux, 1999), 77.
2. Dallas Willard, *The Divine Conspiracy: Rediscovering Our Hidden Life in God* (New York: HarperOne, 1997), 93–94.

Chapter 11: The Road

1. C. S. Lewis, *Mere Christianity* (New York: HarperOne, 2001), 206.
2. One of Peterson's most famous books uses this phrase as its title: Eugene Peterson, *A Long Obedience in the Same Direction* (Downers Grove, IL: InterVarsity, 2000).

Chapter 12: The Defense

1. Screwtape's twelfth letter to Wormwood, in C. S. Lewis, *The Screwtape Letters* (repr., New York: HarperOne, 2001), 57.
2. Timothy Keller, *Walking with God through Pain and Suffering* (New York: Dutton, 2013), 61.
3. A. J. Swoboda, *A Glorious Dark* (Grand Rapids: Baker, 2014), 33.

Chapter 13: The Promise

1. As quoted in Doris E. Curtis and Bryan C. Curtis, *Inspirational Thoughts to Warm the Soul* (Bloomington, IN: iUniverse, 2011), 67.
2. Hays explores this concept of Acts as a book of power in Richard Hays, *The Moral Vision of the New Testament* (New York: Harper One, 1996), 200–04.
3. C. S. Lewis, *The Weight of Glory* (repr., New York: HarperOne, 2001), 42–43.

ACKNOWLEDGMENTS

This book would not have happened without the loving, steady encouragement of my wife, Ali. When I sheepishly shared this idea along with some fragments of chapters, she pushed me to show it to more people and told me to go through with this crazy process. Ali is my constant support and the loving wife I don't deserve, but God has blessed me with her. She has been able to do all of this alongside of finishing medical school and becoming a doctor. She's amazing—I love you, babe.

The second person I showed the partial manuscript to was my friend, the talented writer and editor, Paul Pastor. Without Paul, I am quite sure I would not be the writer I am today and for that, many thanks.

Thank you to Dr. J. Ryan Lister and Dr. Gerry Breshears for their careful edits on early drafts and for helping me think through all of the theological implications of most of what I have said here. Your time and energy is greatly appreciated and I cannot thank you both enough. Western Seminary provided a place for many discussions on this topic and I am so grateful to be a part of such a stellar institution.

Thanks to Natalie Mills and Randall Payleitner at Moody Publishers for their support even before we signed any papers. Your interest and care demythologized the publishing process and got me excited about getting my ideas out there.

To Don, Blair, and Marty at D. C. Jacobson, thank you for believing in me and caring not just about the ideas and the numbers, but about me as a writer, pastor, and person. I am fortunate to have your agency on my side and can't wait for the future.

I would not have written this book without the inspiration and support of my remarkable church family, Willamette Christian Church. To my many mentors, but especially Joel Dombrow and Jon Furman, I am so thankful for you guys in my life. Thanks for teaching me what it means to be a pastor and for being gracious with my shortcomings.

Thank you to my students and my crazy Wednesday Night family, including all of my amazing volunteer leaders and servants who make each night possible. All of you—students and adults alike—show me the grace of Jesus Christ through the lives you all live. If you are currently or have ever been a part of Wednesday Night, please know that you have inspired me to write this book. In many ways, this one's for you.

To Mom and Thomas, I cannot thank you enough. From the beach cabin, to the many amazing dinners, and the countless words of encouragement, you guys continue to bless Ali and me in new ways. I am overwhelmed mostly, however, by your constant prayers. Thank you for showing us what generosity looks like.

Grandma and Grandpa, thank you for charting the path and teaching me the endless blessings of a life in God's presence. And thank you for praying for me as much as you do. I'm convinced much of my life is a result of your careful prayers for me.

Lastly, God has been so good to me. I thank Him for everything, including this book.

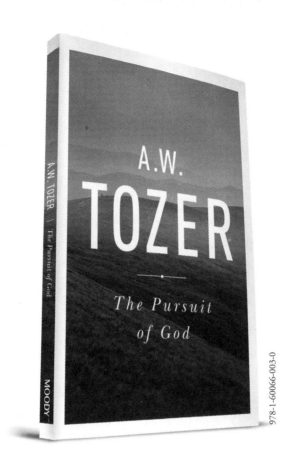

The late pastor and evangelist A. W. Tozer brings the mystics to bear on modern spirituality, grieving the hustle and bustle and calling for a slow, steady gaze upon God. With prophetic vigor and flowing prose, he urges us to replace low thoughts of God with lofty ones, to quiet our lives so we can know God's presence. He reminds us that life apart from God is really no life at all.

also available as an ebook

MOODY
Publishers™

From the Word to Life

More from

moody
collective

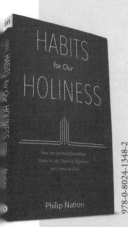

978-0-8024-1348-2

978-0-8024-0652-1

978-0-8024-0624-8

978-0-8024-0857-0

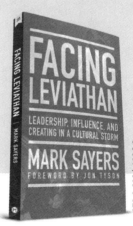

978-0-8024-1096-2

Also available as ebooks

RADICAL

WITH DAVID PLATT

Radical with David Platt, a half-hour national teaching program, airs daily on Moody Radio. Bestselling author, sought-after conference speaker, and pastor, David Platt brings to each program solid, passionate Bible teaching aimed at equipping and mobilizing Christians to make disciples among the nations so that the Lord receives the glory due His name.

www.radicalwithdavidplatt.org

MOODY
Radio™

*From the Word **to Life***